Doctors

Kate hung up, but her fantasy continued. She couldn't get Macklin Riley out of her mind – and she didn't want to. Why was she daydreaming about a man she hardly knew? The Ascot was an ugly, impersonal building which embodied all the greed and power of New York real-estate developers. Why did it seem interesting and glamorous to buy an apartment there? And why was she so intent on Macklin Riley sexually? She was married, and he certainly wasn't particularly handsome. In fact, she couldn't even really remember what he looked like. He came from the strata of society that David always called 'the element'. Was it the power of his position at the hospital that attracted her? The contrast between the friendly way he treated her and the indifference and rudeness with which she and her father had been treated there two years before? Nothing else in the world seemed real except Dr Macklin Riley and his soft, deep voice and his blue, blue eyes.

Also by Susan Cheever

Looking for Work
A Handsome Man
The Cage
Home Before Dark

· *Doctors and Women* ·

SUSAN CHEEVER

Methuen · Mandarin

A Mandarin Paperback

DOCTORS AND WOMEN

First published in Great Britain 1988
by Methuen London
This edition published 1989
by Methuen · Mandarin
Michelin House, 81 Fulham Road, London SW3 6RB

Mandarin is an imprint of the Octopus Publishing Group

Copyright © 1987 by Susan Cheever

Printed and bound in Great Britain
by Cox & Wyman Ltd, Reading

Cheever, Susan, *1943*–
Doctors and women.
I. Title
813'.54[F]

ISBN: 0 7493 0033 7

Grateful acknowledgement is given for the following:

The three paragraphs appearing on page 147 from 'Introductory to the Carcinoma of the Endiometrium,' from *Cancer: Principles and Practice of Oncology*. Copyright © 1982 by J. B. Lippincott. All rights reserved. Used by permission of the publisher.

The Poem 'Places, Loved Ones' by Philip Larkin is reprinted from *The Less Deceived* by permission of the Marvell Press, England

Publisher's Note: This is a work of fiction. Where the name of an actual person or place appears, the respective situation, incident, or dialogue is not intended to depict any actual event or change the entirely fictional nature of the book. While the book depicts medically realistic situations and practices, it is not intended to provide medical advice or illustrate actual medical procedure.

This book is sold subject to the condition
that it shall not, by way of trade or otherwise,
be lent, resold, hired out, or otherwise circulated
without the publisher's prior consent in any form
of binding or cover other than that in which it is
published and without a similar condition
including this condition being imposed
on the subsequent purchaser.

For my mother

· I ·

'You know, we don't talk much anymore,' Kate said. She sprawled on the blue sofa against the windows. David sat upright in a wooden chair holding a book in front of him as he read. He wore a gray tweed jacket, and its leather elbows rested on the heavy mahogany table they had inherited when his parents died.

'Hmmm?' He looked up. His book, Fernand Braudel's history *The Mediterranean*, stayed in place. Although David worked at Loomis, Weiss – the law firm their fathers had started together after the war and Harvard – his first love had always been history.

'I said we don't talk much anymore,' Kate repeated in a slightly louder, slightly exasperated voice. She often complained that David didn't listen to her, or that he didn't hear what she said. He often complained that she mumbled.

Kate dog-eared her paperback copy of *Middlemarch* and closed it, letting it drop to the floor. Beyond her bare feet, out past the curtains, the lights of Manhattan glittered in the lurid night sky. Floodlights caught the grimy spire of St. Jean Baptiste and highlighted the gold knob at the top of the Carlyle hotel.

'We don't have to talk; we know each other very well,' her husband said. In the decade since they had been married, David had often joked that he and Kate knew each other better than they knew themselves. Once this had been comforting and clever, but now it was irritating. It was a ridiculous comment, but in a horrible way it was true. Their fathers, Gideon Loomis and Sam Weiss, had been close friends and partners. David and

Kate were only children, and they were the same age. Although the Loomises had lived in Westchester and the Weisses on Park Avenue in Manhattan, the families had seen each other often, always spent holidays together, and usually summered together in New Hampshire.

In retrospect it often seemed that Kate and David had always been together, or known that they would be together. They had been friends since their earliest memories, and they had survived together the strains of adolescence, the discovery of sex, Kate's automobile accident, the deaths of three of their four parents, and a lot of other things.

Just lately Kate had been feeling that because of all this, her marriage didn't really count. She and David had inherited each other, the way they had inherited money, furniture, and a set of attitudes and behavior. She had never even slept with anyone else, except Ricardo. She had not had to go out into the cold, complicated world, and search for a man who would love her and want to marry her as other girls had to. Her world had provided him.

'Do you think we'll just go on understanding each other? What if one of us changes? What if one of us *has* changed?' Kate buried her toes in the fringed velvet cushions at the end of the couch.

'Is this going to be a long conversation? Should I put down my book?' David marked his place with a bookmark and lay Braudel on the polished surface of the table. 'Why should one of us change?'

'I don't know, don't you think people change sometimes? God, I think I've changed. Daddy dying certainly changed me, and now my mother . . . I mean I hope I've changed. Look how many of our friends are divorced, separated, do you think marriage can just last for decades or . . .'

'My parents' did, you parents' did. What makes you think we're going to be like our friends? What are you talking about, Kate?'

'I think maybe I'm upset about my father. I've been thinking about him a lot.'

'Still?'

'I can't get it out of my mind lately.' That sweltering summer air, the dark upstairs bedroom, her father on the flowered pillows struggling hard for each breath. The syringe which she pushed through the rubber pad of the little, glass morphine bottle, and then into the papery skin of her father's thigh. David and her mother and the minister standing at the foot of the bed and reciting the Lord's Prayer. Thy kingdom come. Thy will be done.

'It's more than two years ago, sweetie,' David said.

'I know, but Mom's sick now, it's the same disease. They say it's different, but I don't know.' Kate shrugged her shoulders as if to indicate that she was a hopeless case, that she didn't want to be associated with her own feelings.

'I thought you said that the doctor said she was going to be all right?'

'He said she had about an eighty percent chance of being all right.'

'That's a pretty respectable percentage.'

'Yes, I'm sorry, I'm being silly.' Kate paused and looked past the frayed edge of her pants' cuff at the carved figures and stylized flowers in the red and blue oriental rug.

David picked his book up off the table and turned away to face it again. Kate was left looking at the back of his head and the neatly cut curls of brown hair above the collar of the tweed jacket. His attention was distracted.

'Would you mind if I went out alone sometimes? For dinner or something, the way you go out for business dinners?' Kate asked in the direction of his back.

'Hmmm?' He turned a page.

'Dr. Riley, you know the doctor I went to see about Mom, asked if I could have a drink with him next week, would that be okay? I have the feeling he wants to explain the treatments to me, it might be important. We might have dinner or something.'

'Sure,' David said without turning around, 'maybe it will make you feel better.' He inclined his head and drew the sides of the book toward him like blinders.

It was so easy. She hadn't known it was going to be so easy.

· 2 ·

Later that night, Kate lay in bed staring up at the dark ceiling and counted days. Five since she had gone down to Parkinson Cancer Center and met Dr. Macklin Riley. Seven since Dr. Gross had called from Westchester to say that during a hysterectomy performed on Matilda Loomis, her mother, they had discovered some malignancy. It had been more than seven hundred days since her father died.

Dr. Gross had dispatched Kate downtown with what he called the pathology – the slides from tissues removed during her mother's operation. It was a rainy day; when she told the cabbie the address, he made a sour face.

'I hate to go over there,' he said. 'They say it's catching.'

Parkinson, the Parkinson Hospital and Cancer Center, was a squat, white-brick building between East End Avenue and the East River. One of the world's foremost cancer research and treatment institutes, it was ten blocks north of New York Hospital. Kate hadn't been there since her father's last visit. She and her father had waited hours together in the dim light of the third-floor, outpatient lounge. Time had another quality in the hospital, as if the world outside with its grandfather clocks and slim gold watches had ceased to exist. It was always a shock to walk out the double glass doors and find that a day or a season had passed.

The waiting-room was an arrangement of shiny blue plastic chairs and sofas, punctuated by low tables crowded with worn magazines. *National Geographic*, *Harper's*, *The New Yorker*, *Smithsonian*. Coffee cup rings made dirty halos around a Trobriand Islands woman in a grass skirt, who stared impassively out from one cover at the waiting patients. Gideon Loomis had been terribly weak by that last visit, and he kept falling asleep and slumping down against the molded plastic. Kate was always afraid he might fall. His body had been so frail that it looked as if it could crumble as it hit the floor, settling into a heap of dust and cloth.

The receptionist at the desk was on the telephone. A line of patients, one on crutches, one child in a wheelchair wearing a baseball cap, waited silently while she ordered a chicken salad, tuna on rye, and three regular coffees. Others waited in chairs on both sides of the hall which led to the examining rooms. Some read books or old magazines, some talked to each other in low voices, but most of them just sat there and stared at the wall.

Whenever a door opened, they started and looked up. A nurse might be coming for them, their name might be called. After the next patient had been summoned and led away, they slumped back in their chairs again. Gideon Loomis had waited in those molded-plastic chairs for his consultation appointments, and his radiation appointments, and his conventional chemotherapy, and his experimental chemotherapy. All that time.

'I'm here to see Dr. Riley, Dr. Gross referred me,' Kate told the secretary finally. The secretary's face was framed with dark hair and slashed with red lipstick; large, gold hoops glinted in her ears. She ran a long, red fingernail down a list of names.

'You're not on the list,' she said.

'I know he's expecting me.'

'Well, hon, he didn't put you down. White? It's not here.'

'It's Weiss, double-you ee eye . . .'

'It's still not here.' The red fingernails clicked against the telephone buttons, the shoulders shrugged a dismissal.

'I just want to drop something off for him.' Kate reached into her pocketbook and produced the envelope of slides from Dr. Gross's operation, the pictures of cells gone wrong in her mother's body.

'You can wait over there, maybe he'll take them when he

comes out.' The secretary nodded toward a chair next to a closed door.

'What does he look like?'

'Tall with gray hair.' She hung up the receiver with a hiss of exasperation, as if Kate had personally kept her very important call from going through. Other people waiting peered over anxiously as Kate sat in the chair and looked down at the beige linoleum floor.

'You can't sit there,' a nurse commanded sharply as she rushed by down the hall. The door of another office slammed behind her. Kate stood up and leaned against the wall outside Dr. Riley's office. Through the wood she could hear a man's deep voice. Her bad knee had begun a low, painful throb in time with her heartbeat. She felt as if all her hours of waiting, all her sorrow and anger, somehow hung in the air of the hallway.

Suddenly the office door burst open, and a short woman with a crown of teased, blonde hair hurried out, followed by a tall man in a doctor's white coat. Kate quickly stepped forward.

'Dr. Riley?' She reached out and touched his white sleeve above where a stethoscope hung from his pocket. He was already moving toward the secretary, and his list, and the rows of expectant faces against the wall.

'Yes?' When he turned, Kate saw that Dr. Riley didn't have gray hair at all, but black hair frosted with white. He had a big head, and rough, tanned skin which looked as if he had just come from outdoors instead of from a dreary, windowless, hospital cubicle.

'I have something for you,' she said. As she groped through her purse for the slides, which, of course, she couldn't find now that she wanted them, she noticed that he had stopped and was standing still and watching her.

'Here, wait, I have something for you,' she said again, finally holding out the envelope of slides. Dr. Riley smiled and reached out to touch her gently on the shoulder.

'Is it yourself?' he said.

'They're slides from my mother's operation, Matilda Loomis, Dr. Gross called you about them,' she babbled, but she had heard what he said, and he kept his hand on her shoulder. His attention in this inattentive place made her feel weak, as if all the strength she had summoned to deal with the hospital was unnecessary now. His steady gaze reassured her. On a level with her eyes, she saw the hospital identification badge on his coat, and two black fountain pens clipped to the pocket.

'Come on in here,' he said.

This sign of favor, this special treatment as the other patients looked anxiously at their watches and the reptilian secretary gawked, made Kate feel lighthearted. There was something powerful about the way Dr. Macklin Riley moved as he stepped back to usher her into the examining room, as if childish things and petty concerns had been stripped away by the necessities of life and death. Kate sat across from him while he took the slides and held them up against a light box.

'This is just a look,' he said. 'I'll have pathology examine them under a microscope.' He was a big man, with broad shoulders and a deep, authoritative voice. There was a slight clumsiness to his movement as if he had never quite adjusted to his own height or the length of his arms.

'How old is your mother?'

'Sixty-six. She was having a hysterectomy, and they found this.'

'As Dr. Gross guessed, it looks like adenocarcinoma of the endometrium – a uterine cancer. Was your mother taking any estrogens? Any pills to help with postmenopausal symptoms?'

'Yes, one called Premarin, I think.' Kate remembered her mother saying that the pills made her dizzy sometimes but that they made her feel better. It had been when her father was sick. Kate had urged her to go on taking them if they made her feel better.

'Why?' she asked.

'Estrogens are associated with this disease in post-menopausal women, but this particular kind of tumor responds very well to treatment.'

'Are you saying those pills might have caused the cancer? Dr. Gross prescribed pills which may have made this happen?'

'It's a very routine prescription, and we can't really tell. We didn't know about the connection between estrogen and endometrial cancer until recently – and of course it might have happened anyway.'

'Still!'

'Yes, it may have been a mistake. Doctors do make mistakes . . . except in this hospital.' Dr. Riley chuckled at his own joke.

'What are her chances?' This was a question she had often asked about her father, and it had never been answered. Doctors would tell her that they didn't know, or that it depended, or that every case was different.

'Statistically, if my reading of these slides is correct, there's about an eighty percent chance that she'll be fine,' Dr. Riley said. 'Of course that doesn't mean much if you're in the wrong twenty percent.' Dr. Riley's joking admission that things could go wrong was more reassuring than if he had tried to smooth over the difficulties. 'She should be fine,' he went on. 'I'll be able to tell you more after I get a report from pathology.'

'It's hard for us, my family, because my father . . .'

'Yes, Dr. Gross mentioned that. What your mother has is not the same thing at all, but it's hard not to worry, I know.'

'What happens next?'

'I want to talk to some other doctors. The malignancy was found during a vaginal hysterectomy, there was no abdominal incision, that means that no one was able to examine the tumor in situ. An abdominal operation would have been more appropriate, and we may still recommend one just to see what's going on.'

'Another mistake?'

'Yes and no. Dr. Gross didn't know what he was dealing with when he began. Most doctors don't expect cancer, don't want to find it.' By talking about other doctors, Dr. Riley seemed to be taking her into his confidence. He leaned toward her over his desk and tapped the slides against the blotter. He appeared to have all the time in the world to answer her questions.

'The other operation, would she have it here?'

'Let's not jump ahead. If she does need it, I think it would be best if she was here, yes, but that would be entirely up to you. Let me get some more input on these slides before I shoot my mouth off anymore. Why don't you call me in the morning, and we'll talk about the next step.' Dr. Riley consulted a worn leather appointment book. 'Say about nine? Then I'll have some more time to talk.'

As Kate left the office, she noticed a black cowboy hat sitting on top of a filing cabinet in the corner. Outside, the hall was still crowded with patients waiting to see Dr. Macklin Riley.

· 3 ·

After the clinic, Macklin Riley took the patients' elevators up to pathology on the seventh floor with the envelope of Matilda Loomis's slides. Clinic ran late; it was after six, and the volunteers and the day staff had gone home, but the brightly lit corridors were still crowded with late visitors, nurses, social workers, and doctors doing rounds – each with their entourage of residents, nurses, and one or two medical students or doctors visiting from other hospitals. He nodded to Ed Kantwell in the elevator. They had a case together, a thirty-seven-year-old school teacher with ovarian cancer, but there was a rule against doctors talking in the elevators. Patients or their families might hear something and become unnecessarily upset.

Up on seven he walked down the empty, green corridor, knocked on Gesner's door, and pushed it open. Allan was hunched over one of his microscopes, surrounded by tables piled with papers, slides, and open books. Through the office window, Riley could see the Queens skyline and the oily, turbulent water of the East River. Outdoors, it was spring. He wondered what Kate Loomis was telling her mother, or her husband if she had a husband. He wondered what other patients were doing, Mrs. Goldman, Eddie Gomez, the kid who loved baseball, Dorothy Clay and her cool, powerful daughter.

'Allan?'

'Oh, hi, Mack.' Allan Gesner looked up, picked his wire-rimmed glasses off a table, wiped the lenses on the sleeve of his white coat, and put them on. Gesner was a pale man with thinning hair and a permanent squint from straining to see the invisible under the unreliable lenses of his instruments. Riley liked him, for his black humor and for his unmatched competence in the pathology department. Allan Gesner never got involved with his patients. Every night after work he went straight to his Chevrolet in the doctors' lot across the street and drove home to his wife and children in Scarsdale. Of course, as a pathologist, Riley reminded himself, Allan Gesner rarely saw patients anyway.

'Could you look at some slides for me?'

'It's kind of late, I'm trying to work on this bloody adriamycin dosage stuff, and I promised I'd make it home for dinner tonight, can it wait?'

'I've got a personal interest in the case,' Riley said.

'I've heard that before. I hope she's gorgeous, Mack, I mean I hope we aren't all working overtime for nothing here – hand them over.' Gesner reached for the slides. He shifted his chair to another microscope, took off his glasses again, and slipped the top slide under the lens.

'Why do you always think it's a woman?' Riley laughed, reached over, and softly punched the other doctor on the shoulder.

'Because it always is,' Gesner retorted. 'I'd say this is grade two, adenocarcinoma situated in the endometrium. You probably figured that much out yourself.' He replaced the slide with another. 'Here's some lymphatic involvement. There's a blood vessel here, so there's vascular involvement. About fifty percent penetration of the uterine wall that I can see, but it's on margin here. What's the story?'

'Sixty-six-year-old postmenopausal woman, on estrogen, suffering from stress incontinence, went in for a hysterectomy. They operated vaginally, and when they saw this malignancy, they tidied up and sent her down here.'

'A peek and shriek, hunh?'

Riley laughed. 'Should we do an abdominal operation just to be sure, or do you think we can get away with radiation treatments?'

'I'd say just give her radiation. It doesn't look like a lot of vascular involvement here, but if it's already shed into the bloodstream, it won't matter anyway. An operation isn't going to add much to what you already know. I'd try some brachytherapy. You wanna play squash tomorrow afternoon?'

'Mallory's on my case about those research papers.'

'Research, Jesus, if we did all the research they wanted us to, we wouldn't have time for the patients.'

'Cancer is not going to be cured at the bedside,' Riley cleared his throat, lowered his voice dramatically, and puffed out his chest, imitating the head of the department, who had recently given a lecture on this subject to the staff in the Howells Auditorium. 'Cancer is not going to be cured at the bedside. It is going to be cured in the laboratory.'

'Fuck the patients,' Gesner said. He took off his glasses and sat back in his chair, rotating his thin shoulders to get the kinks out of his back. He massaged the bridge of his nose with thumb and forefinger, pressing out the places where his glasses had left red crescents of irritation on the pale skin.

'Yeah, the trouble is, ha, ha, we're not supposed to.'

'Christ, Mack, calm down. How's Tammy doing?'

'She seems to be doing just fine. Palm Beach last week, California next week. She's signed the papers at least. She says I've turned into a snob and a social climber. Her lawyer says I owe him five thousand dollars.'

'Next time try and marry someone with lots of money,' Gesner said, as he shifted chairs again, put on his glasses, and bent back over his work. 'You're going to need it.'

· 4 ·

Riley walked to Peter Mallory's door and looked in, past the three desks where his secretaries sat during the day. The office was empty. Mallory would be up on the floors, wearing out his resident. Riley found him just bursting out of the stairwell on four. Peter Mallory never took the elevators. He walked so fast that the resident and students following him always looked winded.

As he watched the tall, lanky doctor race toward him, Riley reminded himself that he had every reason to hate Peter Mallory. For one thing, Mallory was his former mentor and teacher, the man who had been responsible for bringing him to Parkinson. Furthermore, he was a surgeon. Most surgeons arrogantly dismissed chemotherapy and radiation – the alternate methods of treating cancer – and this had drawn angry political lines between the surgeons and the rest of the staff. But Mallory was the rare exception, the surgeon who knew a great deal about chemotherapy and radiation; in fact he seemed to know a great deal about everything. He even went so far as to refer his patients to Riley for chemotherapy if surgery was impossible – if the tumor could not be resected – or for the postsurgery chemo called adjuvant chemotherapy.

Mallory's research in many areas had won him international fame and respect, although at forty-five he was only two years older than Riley. Riley sometimes wondered if Mallory's accomplishments made it hard for him to understand other people's shortcomings. But it was impossible not to like Peter Mallory. There was an eagerness in his sharp, terrier-like face, and a willingness to pay absolute attention, that was totally disarming, no matter how pissed off Riley might be. Mallory might be nagging Riley about not having finished his latest paper, or about not having produced enough research – he might even be wondering if Riley belonged at the hospital. But he was still ready to learn from him.

'Peter!' Riley called out, 'I'm glad I caught you.'

Mallory stopped short, and his resident and medical students skidded to a stop behind him.

'I've got a sixty-six-year-old female patient, grade two adenocarcinoma of the endometrium. Gesner says lymphatic involvement, some vascular involvement, fifty percent penetration of the uterine wall. They found it during a vaginal hysterectomy. Do we do an abdominal or just radiation?'

'Estrogen?' Mallory asked. Although he hardly seemed to have broken stride, he had grasped the situation, weighed the case, and reminded Riley of the information he had left out.

'Yes, Premarin, discontinued a year ago.'

'I'd say no operation if Gesner agrees,' Mallory was already moving down the hall, his white-coated companions strung out behind him. 'Who needs it.'

'Thanks,' Riley said.

'Eddie Gomez is back,' Mallory said, louder, since he was halfway down the hall by now. 'Go see him.'

Riley didn't have to be told to go see Eddie Gomez, the ten-year-old kid with leukemia up in the pediatrics ward on five. Eddie wasn't a patient of Riley's. He had met the little boy one weekend when he covered the pediatrics ward for Dave Kinsey. The kid's spirit and his fascination with baseball, with his own treatment, with every kind of knowledge, had touched a lot of the doctors, Riley in particular.

'I see you're back in time for baseball season,' Riley told him, as he swung into the big room where Eddie's mother sat reading to him. The Gomezes were a family from Santo Domingo, who had lived in New York for a decade. Eddie had first come into the hospital at the end of the winter, hoping to be accepted for a bone marrow transplant. He had the wrong kind of disease for that, and they had sent him home for a while – he had even insisted on going back to school. Now he was back.

'School's out,' Eddie said, 'I didn't have anything else to do but come and cheer you guys up.'

'You don't have to cheer me up,' Riley said. 'The Mets are doing that.'

'Great, aren't they great? Did you see what I got yesterday?' Eddie took a worn baseball cap down from the bedpost. 'Dad got it for me, he's a friend of some bigshot at Shea Stadium.' Handling the hat as if it was a sacred object, Eddie proferred it to Riley. 'It's Tom Seaver's hat,' he said, 'one he really wore. See?'

'Wow, that's a treasure, your dad must have told him some stories about what a terrific kid you are.'

'My dad can make me sound pretty good,' Eddie said. Riley flipped the cap onto Eddie's head. The smooth-skinned, little boy's face peered out from under the visor.

'See you later, alligator,' Riley said.

Back in his own office, Riley dumped his weary body into his chair and contemplated his stack of message slips. He wanted to go home, although when he thought about the little room piled with packing crates that would be his home until he moved, he felt even worse. Quickly he shuffled through the pink message slips, as if there might be something there to lighten his spirits. Mr. Donaldson had abdominal pains. Mrs. Ingall's leg was worse. Janet Owsley had trouble breathing. Would he write another prednisone prescription for Annie Golden? Barbara Morse was having a bad reaction to the adriamycin – her doctor had called. Dorothy Clay wanted to know if she should come in next week. Ann Lacey had called, no message. He reached over the telephone to an open box of fancy chocolates in the shape of sports equipment, the latest of the gift boxes from patients. He set aside the baseball for Eddie and bit into the chocolate tennis racket. In his mouth, it tasted like sawdust. Still chewing, he began to dial the first of his calls.

· 5 ·

'You look great,' David said, 'your body is so pink.' Kate had just walked into the bedroom from the bathroom where she had taken a long, dreamy hot bath. There was a blue towel wrapped around her, and bits of bubble still stuck to her back and arms like scraps of cloud.

'Can I give you a back rub?' David asked. This was his euphemism for sex. If she said yes, he would start by massaging her back, and then when her body started to move under his hands, he would spread her legs and take her from behind.

'Sure,' Kate said. She had been looking forward to slipping between the clean sheets and reading and then deliciously falling asleep. Now she stepped over to David's side of the bed. Reluctantly, she felt her body warming in expectation. It was amazing to her how little she could like David, and how much she could still like fucking him. He always had to ask her if she wanted to have sex, and there was always some ploy like the back rub. Why couldn't he just say, 'Come here, I want you,' or even just, 'Strip' the way men did in her fantasies.

Kate lay with her stomach down against the cool sheets and opened her legs so that he could kneel between them.

'We haven't fucked forever,' she said, stretching up against the pillows.

'I know, I thought maybe you had fallen out,' David said.

'I haven't fallen out, I still love you.' But Kate's irritation grew with her excitement. There was always this litany of insecurity and reassurance. With each upward stroke of his hands, he bumped against her jaw. His clumsiness made her angry, and for a moment she felt like turning around and slapping him.

'Mmmmm,' he said, 'that feels good.' Slowly, as if he didn't want her to notice because he was afraid she might change her mind, he eased her legs apart with his knees. With each stroke of the massage now, he brought his hands farther round the front of her body towards her breasts. Kate pushed herself up against the pillows and back against his body. He brought his hands around and gently rubbed her nipples. Her irritation seemed to add to the excitement, she moved her buttocks back and forth against him, and David took a hand off her breasts and reached down to put himself inside her. She reared up toward him, wanting him to touch her everywhere, to have her completely, to do everything to her.

'Come on,' she said. She pushed him off with her buttocks and turned over, reaching down to stroke him before she put him back inside her.

Kate often had fantasies during sex with David – fantasies about other men or other men and women. Suddenly she wondered what it would be like if Dr. Riley was on top of her instead of her husband, and she felt a surge of pleasure. He was so big, so commanding, he seemed to know everything. She imagined his broad body, his long arms, the way he would tell her what to do. Then she was angry at herself. It was wrong to fantasize about someone else, particularly her mother's cancer doctor, Jesus! She felt herself beginning to come. She pushed herself up toward him, pushing until she didn't think about anything anymore. He was inside her, his hands on her breasts, his mouth on her mouth, he was coming. It didn't matter who was on top of her now. Kate's body took on its own movements, her mind filled with stars, an image of a waterfall, a delicious blankness, and then it was over, and silent David was lying in her arms again.

Later that night, as she slept beside David on the queen-sized mattress they had bought when they were married, Kate dreamed about Dr. Macklin Riley. Light from a full moon slanted in through the venetian blinds onto the bed, and the rumble of trucks ten floors below in the street came in through the open window with the warm night air. Occasionally the noise of sirens and the bleeping honk of fire engines pulsed through the low hum of traffic noise, interrupted by the rhythmic racket of the garbage trucks – the clang of the cans, the crunch as the garbage was heaved into the back of the truck, the whine of the compactor.

In the dream, Kate and David were at an opening for members at the Museum of Modern Art. They were wearing evening clothes. David had on a dinner jacket with the crystal studs her father had given him, and Kate her black and silver dress that a saleslady had talked her into buying, and that she loved now, and they were standing around at the top of the stairs eating smoked salmon and making polite conversation.

It was a summer evening, in the dream, and Kate could see the trees and statues of the garden court through the glass walls. Suddenly she looked over Alden Higgenbotham's right shoulder and saw that Dr. Macklin Riley was there. He was driving an open jeep which he had somehow brought up in the freight elevator, a red jeep, and he was wearing the black cowboy hat. He roared past them, the prim assembled gathering of art patrons, gunning the engine, through the drawing exhibits, down past the big Monet, and around the corner toward the Matisse bathers.

No one spoke as he drove by. Kate wanted to run after him in her tight dress and her absurd high heels. She wanted to sit next to him in the speeding jeep and have him sweep her away from the artificial manners and traditional constraints of her life with David – of her life, period. Instead, after he was gone and she hadn't followed him, she turned and asked Mr. Higgenbotham if he didn't think this was a lovely party.

· 6 ·

Kate was tall, she always thought too tall, with thick, dark brown hair and eyes in a full face. Although she had been told she had a wonderful smile, although the mirror reflected a woman she would have admired herself, she often wished she were more distinguished looking, more special. The one special thing about her was a liability; she walked with a slight limp, the physical memory of an evening in 1966 when her father had been driving her home from a country club dance along Route 9 in Tarrytown. An oncoming car had veered toward them, and in order to avoid a collision, Gideon Loomis had yanked the wheel of the big Buick to the right, slamming the car into the low stone wall of the Sleepy Hollow Cemetery.

Kate had been miserable at the dance. It was always a relief when her father picked her up in his big car. The strain of lying to him, of pretending that he was an ordinary father picking up his pretty daughter after a gay dance, just like on television, was so much less than the strain of standing at the edge of the shiny dance floor, watching the other girls twirl and giggle, smiling until it hurt, and pretending to have a great time about nothing.

Kate had friends at school, in her classes, at study hall, but the same girls, who seemed to be her peers as they all banged through the corridors of Langley Hall in blue serge uniforms, were suddenly transformed on the dance floor. They became glittering creatures, animated and chattering, creatures who made cute faces at boys and pretended there was nothing more important in the world than some idiot's problems on the football team or the color of a new nail polish. They were different, Kate was the same. Behind her false smile, she stood, partnerless, and analyzed the girls spinning by to Lester Lanin's big-band sound. Some were plainer than she was, or fatter. Others wore homemade dresses or had messy hair or sulky faces. Still, they had something – something which Kate didn't have, or couldn't get, and couldn't even really identify.

David, the only man who ever did flirt with her or ask her to dance, did it because he had to. He had been shipped off to boarding school in Massachusetts. She was just as happy he didn't have the opportunity to see her standing at the edge of the dance floor, waiting for each dance to be over and the soft applause of the dancers so that she could start hoping again.

When she came to after the accident, there was the taste of rust in her mouth and the sticky warmth of blood, and everything hurting, and bright lights shining in her eyes, and she thought, well, maybe I won't have to go to dances anymore.

Then there were the doctors. Doctors for her torn skin, and doctors for her severed nerves, and even a psychiatrist. Dr. Jonas, her pediatrician, had told her parents she would never walk again. Although no one told Kate about this, she could see the fear in her parents' faces as they bent over her hospital bed day after day – and she knew that they were wrong. That kind of thing wasn't going to happen to her. Dr. Sobell at Columbia-Presbyterian was more encouraging. Finally, after her grandfather got involved, she went to Dr. Fred Brennan at New York Hospital.

Fred Brennan was a friendly older man with a mane of white hair and a fatherly manner that made Kate feel safe and cared for. He was also the best orthopedic-rehabilitation man in the country. Together Kate and Dr. Brennan, through therapy, hard work, and another operation, restored most of her leg's function. Even years after the accident, when she had had trouble again, Dr. Ricardo Charles had been able to straighten it out fairly easily, although it was hardly worth it considering what Ricardo did to the rest of her life.

The accident had changed Kate in ways she couldn't measure. It kept her from going off to boarding school. Instead, she continued as a day student at Langley Hall. At the time this seemed like a good idea, but later Kate was left with the feeling that she hadn't gone to a very good school, that her schooling was second-rate. And the injury and her crutches had won her a grudging kind of special treatment from her schoolmates. More than that, it reassured her that she would be able to overcome anything. Kate had always felt special and powerful as a child. For years she had believed that, if she really wanted to, she could fly. The accident, and her victory over her own body, reinforced this secret idea. She was going to be able to control her own life.

Now, years later, fading scars and the odd shape of one knee were all that remained of the injuries which had kept her in a cast or on crutches for a year. There were still things she couldn't do. But she had even taught herself a lopsided jog which she practiced some mornings on the Central Park track. And when she had finally married David, seven years after the accident, and five years after his conversion, they had walked down the aisle of All Saints as straight and clear-eyed as any other exemplary, young Episcopalian couple.

Years later, when Kate found out that her father had a drinking problem, and years after that when she learned what it meant to be an alcoholic, she was left with a question about that night which she could never answer, and that her father probably wouldn't have been able to answer even if she had had the nerve to ask him. There was no evidence and no reliable memory to go by. The man in the other car, the car which Gideon Loomis said had forced him to swerve into the wall, was never prosecuted – if he should have been. The police had no records outside of the descriptive facts on the accident report. Gideon Loomis was a well-known citizen in Westchester, a leader of civic clubs, a former chairman of the Board of Legislators, a trustee of Hudson College. When the police found him struggling to get out of his wrecked car it was, 'Yes, Mr. Loomis, let me help you, sir, the ambulance is on its way, Mr. Loomis.' They certainly weren't about to ask any stupid questions.

· 7 ·

Of all the things Dr. Macklin Riley had discussed with Kate that first afternoon, the one that she remembered and fretted about that night and early the next morning was the possibility that her mother might have to have another operation. Her mother would be just another patient then, shuffling down the linoleum hallways in a loose, frayed hospital gown, pushing an IV pole, just like her father had. Matilda Loomis looked healthy now, but then her body would be thin, her skin would take on a waxy sheen, and that would be the beginning of the long ending. How could that happen to them?

Gideon Loomis's death had been the end of many things, but there was still the house with its thick, old copper beeches and sloping lawns and familiar rooms and the family gatherings at Christmas and Thanksgiving. There was still somewhere to go, someone to ask if you needed things – whether or not you would get them. Kate and her mother had always been distant but friendly. Her passion had been reserved for her father. Now Kate realized that she could afford to be distant from her mother only because she thought that her mother would always be there.

If Matilda was gone, Kate would have no family at all. Now she regretted not having a brother or sister. David was a frail and inadequate bulwark against the world. They would sell the house and auction off the furniture except for a few things. They would have to clean out the attic and get rid of the shelves of toys and books from Kate's childhood. The wicker rocking chair she had sat on as a little girl, the worn brown bear on wheels, the piles of colored wooden blocks, the blue bicycle.

Out would go the college art projects, and the mementos from trips abroad or to the Caribbean, and the rugs and paintings and furniture that no one wanted, but no one wanted to part with.

At exactly nine in the morning, Kate dialed the number Dr. Riley had given her. It took four calls and half an hour to get through. She was frustrated and impressed.

'Hello, Dr. Riley, this is Kate Weiss.'

'Hi, it's nice to hear your voice,' he said.

'So, what's the verdict?' Kate thought of the second operation as a terrible punishment for her and for her mother – a punishment which Dr. Riley could inflict or commute.

'The verdict?'

'Do you think my mother needs a second operation?'

'Oh, that verdict.' He laughed. 'As you know, Kate, your mother originally had a vaginal hysterectomy, there was some question of another operation being advisable, an abdominal exploration. I met with Dr. Allan Gesner, who's the head of pathology, and had a conference with Dr. Peter Mallory, one of our top surgeons.' Dr. Riley spoke in the deep official doctor voice Kate had first heard through his office door. 'Your mother has what we call a grade-two disease. We have no evidence that it has spread, and so at this time the consensus seems to be that another operation isn't necessary.'

Kate felt a wave of relief. 'No operation?'

'That's right, the risks of an abdominal operation at this time, although they aren't great, outweigh the other risks. We would recommend a series of radiation treatments.'

'Where would she have them?' Kate felt giddy, lightheaded.

'She could have them at Westchester Hospital if that's more convenient. It isn't necessary for her to have them here. I could set that up for you.'

'But would it be safer if there was another operation? I mean are you sure it's okay?' Kate cursed her own ingratitude, questioning this wonderful man, who only wanted to help her.

'As sure as we can be. If there is any tumor in the regional lymph nodes, the radiation should take care of it. The radiologist will probably want to use some brachytherapy. That's a process of using a radiation implant near the affected organs.'

'Phew,' Kate whistled, finally, 'that's very good news.' She was sitting at the desk in her office, but her body seemed to be floating. Outside she could see the black, cylindrical shapes of the chimneys above the brick building across the street, and the stained barrel of the water tower on the next building. In the distance to the south, beyond some square, brick chimneys and the top floors of a white-brick apartment building, a silver plane moved through wisps of high clouds.

'I knew you'd be relieved,' he said. His voice was low and certain, and she could hear his radio in the background. The strains of a Beethoven piano concerto seeped through the receiver along with the warmth and reassurance she felt from Macklin Riley.

'Well, thank you, really, you've been wonderful,' Kate said, 'you've really helped, more than I can say.'

'That's my job,' Riley said.

'I know, but it usually doesn't get done, I'm very grateful.'

'Jack Gross mentioned that you're a writer, that sounds interesting,' he said.

'I'm just a journalist, really, it's not a big deal. My husband says I make just enough money to put us in a higher tax bracket.'

'It's a big deal to someone like me, I have a lot of trouble writing. What do you write about? Where do you get your ideas?'

'Well, right now I'm writing about a German artist,' she said. 'The piece was an editor's idea, or at least he thinks it was. Usually I get the ideas, and then I try to get the editors to think that they thought of them – it works better that way.'

Riley laughed. 'I know what you mean, it's that way around here too. I'm collecting some art myself, some paintings, maybe you'd like to come and look at them, I'm in the process of moving, so things are a little confused right now.'

'Where are you moving to?' Kate wondered how many calls

were on hold, how many patients were calling and getting the busy signal, and how many urgent messages were stacking up on Riley's desk.

'A building called The Ascot, have you heard of it? I've just signed a contract on an apartment there.' The Ascot was a glass and steel plinth jutting out of a block of brownstones southeast of where Kate and David lived. A sliver building, on a tiny lot, it was forty stories high and towered over the rest of the neighborhood. A dozen tall, narrow slivers had been built in Manhattan in the past decades, most of them on the Upper East Side where real estate values had increased ten or twenty times, and The Ascot was the most luxurious and pretentious of all of them. Kate and David had joked about its full-page ads in the newspaper, which offered a white Rolls-Royce to whoever bought the penthouse, and which included flowery paeans to the neighborhood – the very neighborhood it would destroy.

'The Ascot, that sounds fabulous, of course I've heard of it,' Kate said.

'Would you like to come by and see the apartment sometime?'

'Sure, I'd be fascinated. I don't know anyone else who has even looked at an apartment there.'

'I don't like to do what everyone else does.'

'You're a fugitive from the law of averages,' Kate said, but Macklin Riley didn't laugh.

'I like to be different If I can,' he said.

'Did you and your wife look at a lot of apartments?'

'No, as a matter of fact we're separated, that's one of the reasons for the move.'

'I'm sorry,' Kate said.

'Well, I'm not.' Riley laughed loudly at his own wit. 'I had, still have, a studio on Third Avenue, and we had a house near Philadelphia where she works. We saw each other on weekends . . . when I didn't have to work.'

'She put up with that? Sounds like the perfect marriage.'

'Not exactly,' but now Riley laughed again as if she had said something quite funny. 'Anyway, why don't you come up and see the apartment next week? We can have dinner.'

'I can't have dinner,' Kate said, 'I'm married.'

'Married people don't eat?'

Kate laughed. 'Actually my husband goes off to business dinners without me sometimes, it's just that I never have.'

'A double standard. Now there's the perfect marriage!'

'All right, all right, I guess I can have dinner.'

'Let me call you later,' Riley said, 'I'd like to talk some more about all this, in the meantime why don't you set up the radiation appointments with Dr. Harris in Westchester? He will have talked to me, okay?'

'Okay.' Kate tried hard to remember what Dr. Macklin Riley looked like. There was the black and white hair and his bigness, but she couldn't bring his features into focus in her memory. The half hour she had spent with him at the hospital only yesterday seemed indistinct and long ago. There was the black cowboy hat. The Dr. Riley in her dream was more vivid, the dashing outlaw with the bright red jeep. He would wear jeans and high boots and swagger a little as he showed her around his apartment at The Ascot. He was supremely confident; he was starting a new life. Standing next to him, she would look down at the rest of the world, small and far away. This will be the living room, he would say, and this will be the bedroom. His black cowboy hat would lie in a pool of sunlight on the polished floor in the empty room, and the late afternoon sun would slant in through high windows. Her mother was going to be all right.

· 8 ·

Their apartment building was a redbrick, twelve-story prewar at a corner of Lexington Avenue in the eighties, with white granite lozenges along the lintels, and a frieze of lions' heads along the top, glaring down at the street. When Sam Weiss had bought the apartment for his son and new daughter-in-law, buying a cooperative apartment had been an eccentric idea. Everyone else was still renting. Kate felt a combination of relief and apprehension when he had presented the stock certificates to them over dinner at the old Canari d'Or. They would have somewhere to live. That was good. They would be tied forever to the Upper East Side and the life they had grown up in. That was bad. David didn't seem to mind though. Nothing seemed to suit him better than living out their parents' fantasies, living near them in low-key comfort, going into the law firm after school and rising – not too fast, but just fast enough – to the top. Marrying Kate.

Their living room looked out on the backs of other buildings and the roofs and towers of the Upper East Side. From there Kate could see dozens of other windows, and she liked to watch the lights go on at dusk, the lamplight behind the heavy chintz curtains across the way, and the track lighting in the minimalist apartment to the left of it, and all the other different windows with their different décors and dramas. There were the fighters, who always seemed to be gesticulating wildly at each other until one stomped out of the room and the other sulked morosely on the couch, and the lovers, a man and a woman whose intertwined feet and legs were just tantalizingly visible at the edge of a window with a blue curtain, and Tubehead, the bald man who sat night and day staring at the flickering, silver light of his television set. When Kate was up late, she would wander into the living room and see who else had their lights on, who else was up worrying at two or three in the morning.

Just across the courtyard from their apartment lived a large family whose dining room and children's bedroom faced Kate's windows. At night, when the lights went on, Kate could see the father reading to his son and daughter who sat next to him on the bottom of their bunk-bed, or a cocktail party with men and women holding glasses and standing in uncomfortable groups, or the pretty baby-sitter racing from the bedroom to the living room and back again with her charges screaming and running after her, and all tumbling on the sofa in a heap of hugs and laughter.

At Christmas the family had a big tree with tiny lights and strings of colored balls and an angel on top, and at Easter there were paperwhites in the window and baskets filled with grass and brightly colored eggs. Kate had charted the years and the seasons by the children's growth, from tiny babies in bassinets with starched white nurses, to boisterous six- and eight-year-olds. That was the family she could have had, she thought.

Kate had missed growing up in a large family. Long ago, back in the seventies when there was a population crisis, Kate and David had agreed without too much conversation that having children was an immoral act in a terrible world. It was a decision that Kate hadn't thought about much until she turned thirty. No one they knew well had children, and the few couples they knew who did were always talking about how tough it was, how it changed your life and messed up your marriage, how you could never just spend a day in bed together or spontaneously go out for dinner.

People who had children often seemed older, even if they were the same age – especially the women – and they often looked sort of worn out, their hair ragged, their skin rough, as if they didn't care anymore. But in spite of all the good reasons not to have children, and in spite of all the reasons on which Kate and David had based their decision, Kate was beginning to wonder if she didn't want to have a child after all. Time was forcing her to decide. There was no reason to, she scolded herself. Everything was against it. Still, it was a persistent, small desire, a desire impervious to all the reasons she had, a desire she couldn't talk herself out of. It wasn't that she wanted to do it, she told herself firmly, it was just that she didn't want to miss it, and that was not a good enough reason to want to do it.

A couple of times, since her father's death, she had tried to discuss it with David. 'I thought we had decided not to do that,' he said. She took this as a rejection, and didn't ask again for a long time. The next time she brought it up, his attitude had changed. If she wanted to have children, he said, fine, why didn't she go ahead and have them? She had to do what she had to do. It was all right with him. That wasn't the point, of course. She wanted to talk about whether or not to have children. She wanted someone to decide for her – or at least help her decide. She wanted to talk about her worries and desires. She wanted to talk, period.

Kate felt more and more that her time was running out. Every time she went to the gynecologist, she asked him if it wasn't already too late. No, he said. Life offered her two possibilities. It would be a disaster if she didn't have a child, she would always feel she had missed something; it would heighten her loneliness. She would never know the joys which had been the principal human joys. On the other hand, it would be a disaster if she did have a child. David didn't really want one. She could see his point. She valued her freedom and her free time. During weeks when she hadn't had enough time to herself, she was claustrophobic and cranky. She was afraid that she wouldn't be able to handle a child's incessant demands, and this certainly was confirmed when she was around other people's children. How did they stand it?

Since there was no satisfactory resolution to this problem, Kate had become adept at putting it off. She was thirty-two now. She took comfort from statistics on the increasing age of mothers of first children. She tried to still that insistent, irrational little desire. David didn't mind putting it off. Putting it off had become a way of life.

· 9 ·

Kate's apartment was furnished with David's furniture, because both his parents were dead. Old Sam Weiss had had a heart attack on the tennis court in Palm Beach seven years ago. He was playing doubles in a seniors' tournament, and after the third set he just lay down on the court and couldn't get up. Sam had enjoyed his prosperity intensely, although his swarthy face and shoulders had never looked right in a dinner jacket, even when it was made for him in London, or in tennis whites, or any of the other clothes he wore after he got rich, any more than David's mother, Hilda, looked as if she should be driving the low-slung, red Jaguar with HILDA plates that some slick West Palm Beach salesman had talked them into buying.

Sam Weiss had become an Episcopalian when David was old enough to be confirmed, but it hadn't made any difference. He and his wife were two cozy little people, who could hardly see over the wheel of their car, two people who were most comfortable in their overfurnished living room, sitting on the brocades and stirring coffee *mit schlag* with tiny silver spoons. They were both Viennese, raised in the intimate scale of Europe before the war, a world of Mozart, gooey pastries, and *gemütlich* living arrangements. They had been dwarfed by their tall, athletic American son.

Hilda, David's mother, had died just a few months after her husband. First she had a stroke and then her own heart attack, but her death was clearly the result of not wanting to live alone. David had been terribly hurt by this, although he never talked about it. He took it personally that he, Hilda's only son, was not enough reason for her to stay alive. On the surface, he had taken his parents' deaths calmly. He had been appropriately subdued for a few days, and he had made the telephone calls and the arrangements. His eulogy at the service at St. Thomas was eloquent and moving. After all, Kate and David told each other glibly when the subject came up, Sam and Hilda had both been in their seventies. They had had good lives. They had lived out their dreams. It wasn't like Kate's father.

The Weiss furniture was like its owners, heavyset and close to the ground, with ornate carving and balled feet on everything. Biedermeier chests against the walls, overstuffed couches with matching hassocks, and tables covered with overlapping velvet and paisley cloths which hung to the floor, edged with green silk tassels. Every inch of their walls was hung with oil paintings in gold frames. Ships at sea, horses standing under great elms, children laced into satin clothes with tiny dogs on their laps. Every inch of table surface was covered with objects and bibelots, photographs of the family in silver frames, silver boxes and cups, porcelain bowls of marble fruit, and marble bowls of procelain fruit.

Kate had used a fraction of the Weiss furniture in their apartment – the rest was in storage – but the rooms still seemed crowded. The furniture seemed to mark them forever as children. They had never started out, as their friends did, with a few simple pieces or with nothing and then had to develop a household. From the beginning, their own tastes had been overwhelmed by Sam and Hilda's gifts, and Sam and Hilda's cast offs. Instead of collecting, they had had to pare down.

Before dinner, Kate watched listlessly as David changed from his business suit into chinos and a polo shirt. She sat cross-legged at the end of the bed, absentmindedly braiding a lock of thick hair.

'We're having fish, okay?'

David always sat upright. His body was neat, accommodating to clothes. He had an unselfconscious ease that Kate envied.

'Sounds fine.' He was distracted, concentrating on combing his hair into its perfect waves.

'I went to the fish market,' she said. It had taken five minutes to get a salesman to notice her. They had all been busy serving sleek women in knit suits.

'As long as it's not those dead scallops we had last week.'

'If you have complaints about the food, maybe you'd like to do the shopping.'

'Sure, I'll do it anytime.' The fact that this was true, and that the salesman at the fish store would have waited on trim David in his business suit first, irritated her.

'Anyway,' David said, 'I don't have any complaints, the fish sounds fine.' His face was fresh and clean, his lines impeccable. Why did David always have to be so perfect?

'You *were* complaining, about the scallops. You're so legalistic. Why can't you listen to what I'm saying instead of defending yourself all the time?' Kate felt at a distinct disadvantage – David argued the way he dressed – impeccably.

'I wasn't defending myself, I just made the simple statement that I hadn't complained.'

'Yeah, but you had complained, that's the point. Save your arguing genius for the office, why don't you?'

'Now *you're* being legalistic.'

'That's just what I mean! You didn't even hear what I said.'

'Are you upset about something? It isn't like you to fight over nothing.' David was standing in the doorway now. His sleek looks and cool manner were infuriating. Kate could see that he wanted to go into the kitchen to get his evening beer, but that he was hesitating because he knew that she would be angry if he just turned and walked out of the room. The fight, her feelings, were not important to him. The beer was part of his routine. That was what he cared about. David did not like to have his routine interrupted.

'I'm not picking a fight,' she said. '*You* are being impossible.'

'Can I get you a beer?' he said.

'I don't drink beer, I thought you knew me so well.' Now she heard pure sarcasm in her voice.

'I was just trying to be friendly, you don't make it easy. Maybe you should try a beer.' Kate didn't drink because it made her fat. No matter what David ate or drank, he never gained a pound.

'Okay, I'm sorry, let's just drop it,' she said. But she wasn't sorry at all, she was angry and hurt. It was obvious to her that all David wanted was no trouble, and he didn't care how he got it. Even a stranger like Dr. Riley could understand her better than her own husband.

· 10 ·

The long corridors of doctors' offices at the Parkinson Center are lit all night, although unlike the patients' corridors, where there are the sounds of groans and low voices, they are quiet. It was usually about 5:30 A.M. when the first individual lights went on in the doctors' offices. Dr. Peter Mallory had driven in from his house, leaving New Jersey in darkness and crossing the bridge at dawn. He liked to put in two hours of work on research papers before he made his first rounds at seven. This morning, he was late. Jamie had been sick, and his wife Jane was up two or three times during the night. In the dim light of his bedroom, he could feel her fuming as he slept obliviously through her emergencies. It had been her idea to live in the country, but now she complained that he was never home. It was true. By the time he got to the house at eleven or even later, he needed sleep, needed it overwhelmingly. And there were other people, very sick people, much sicker than he prayed Jamie would ever be, who needed him to have that sleep. Her complaints weren't reasonable, as he often reminded her. She had agreed in marrying him that she would accommodate to his schedule, that she would take care of the house and children. But this just seemed to make her angrier.

This morning he was tired though, more fatigued by the blunt, silent weapon of her resentment than his lack of sleep. He started by signing a pile of letters and notes he had ignored last night. The fatigue would pass. Mallory had learned that he could work right through tiredness to a second or third wind. From the letters, he turned to the word processor and pushed the disk for his research on monoclonal antibody treatments for malignant cutaneous melanoma into the drive. The charts and documents were almost done, but although he didn't dwell on it, Mallory knew that the results weren't promising.

Melanoma was an ugly disease, he hated it as if it were a personal enemy. It seemed as if he had done a million wide excisions, cutting away the skin around the black stain, sectioning the tumor for pathology, fixing the skin graft, and yet the disease often continued in spite of his work. It struck the young and the old, it didn't care. First an odd, irregular nevus, then the positive nodes and the long, losing battle.

It was eight o'clock in the morning by the time Mallory picked up two residents at the elevator bank and ran upstairs to the twelfth floor. He could feel energy coming back as he started moving again. His body was an optimist. One of the residents, the new one in the pink shirt, started panting after the first flight of stairs, and noticing this, Mallory increased his sprinting speed. He was in full swing by the time he raced through the staff room at the entrance to the nurses' station. Each floor at Parkinson had a staff room and a nurses' station with shelves for the patients' charts at the center of the floor, and patients' rooms around the circumference of the floor on the other side of the corridor.

'Medicine by committee,' Mallory snorted as he raced past a group of doctors bent over a chart in the staff room. The thin resident smiled. Good, maybe he would be more than a liability. Each month, Mallory was assigned two residents, men and women who had graduated from medical school and had to be called doctors, but who sometimes had less on the ball than his eight-year-old son, Jamie. Heads turned as Mallory strode into the nurses' station; his sandy hair stood on end as if activated by the electricity he generated. Two of the nurses drifted toward him.

'Get the charts.' The residents pulled a series of loose-leaf notebooks out of their cubbyholes. Everyone looked sleepy. One of the nurses' hair was still wet from her morning shower. The resident had a residue of crust around one eye.

'Two codes last night,' a nurse said. 'There weren't any "Do

Not Resuscitate" orders, so we went through the whole thing. They're both in intensive care now.'

'Oh that's great, wonderful!' Mallory said. Dying patients were often resuscitated when he thought they should have been allowed to die. The resuscitation process itself was difficult and brutal, ribs were broken. And for what? Usually the patient lived less than a week, hooked up to the expensive machines down in the intensive care unit.

A few years ago it had been different. When Mallory had first come to Parkinson, there had been symbols on each chart which told the nurses how to respond in the event that a patient stopped breathing. A white dot was the code meaning that the patient should be resuscitated. Red was the color if the patients had formally agreed, or if the family had agreed, that they should not be resuscitated. Blue was the 'slow code.' In these cases of patients who would be beyond help in their doctor's opinion, it was arranged so that the resuscitation teams would come too slowly to do any good. Purple had been the 'show code' for patients whose families insisted that they be resuscitated although the doctor judged it useless. In these cases, the team would try unsuccessfully to revive the patient. All that was changed now, after a few complaints and a few stories in the newspapers. Now everyone had to be resuscitated unless they or a family member had signed a form agreeing otherwise. The hospital was afraid of lawsuits.

The lawyers and reporters who had changed things didn't have any idea what it was like to get consent for 'Do Not Resuscitate' orders. Mallory wished that some of them had the task of trying to explain to a sick, anxious patient that, really, it would be best if they weren't revived. Sometimes the patients and their families didn't speak English. It was hard to bring up the subject with patients who weren't very sick and didn't expect to die, and it was equally hard to bring it up with patients who were sick and thought they might die.

Mallory had sidestepped the 'Do Not Resuscitate' problem by just trying not to be around. In theory all patients who were admitted to the hospital had a little talk with their doctor about whether or not they chose to be resuscitated. Then the doctor wrote the appropriate orders on their charts. But many of the doctors didn't have the time or the inclination to have these little talks. What happened instead was that all patients got resuscitated, even if they were going to die anyway – even if they were clearly ready to die. You had to beg to be left alone in your last moments, beg to be allowed to go. The situation was ridiculous, Mallory thought, a typical case where fear instead of compassion or good medicine created the rules.

He perched at the edge of a desk and the residents were joined by another nurse and a tall doctor, Macklin Riley. Mallory knew that Riley didn't have time to sit and gab in the nurses' station.

'Okay, here's your joke for the morning,' Mallory began. Riley's beeper went off and he moved away. 'The internist is the doctor who knows about everything and *does* nothing. The psychiatrist is the doctor who *thinks* he knows everything . . . and doesn't tell anything.' (Peter Mallory didn't believe that psychiatrists knew much of anything, but a joke is a joke.) 'The pathologist is the doctor who knows everything . . . a day too late.' One of the nurses began to giggle. 'And the surgeon is the doctor who knows nothing . . . and does everything.' Everyone laughed. Another resident wandered over to see what the fun was about. Mallory jumped off the desk.

'Tell the one about the duck!' one of the nurses asked.

'Not today, troops, let's go,' and Mallory was off down the hall. As he walked, he flipped through a stack of index cards covered with names and notes. Mrs. Rosen was scheduled for her operation tomorrow. Mr. Webster was recovering nicely. Angela was still on the IV. Damn, Peter Mallory thought, he hoped he wasn't going to have to fire Macklin Riley.

Mrs. Rosen was the first room across from the nurses' station, a forty-five-year-old, Long Island housewife with two children. Abdominal pains and weight loss had sent her to her family doctor, who told her not to worry. Now she had a tumor as big as a fist in her lower abdomen, but on the CAT scan it looked as if it could be removed surgically. This would be the kind of operation Mallory liked, clean with almost certain positive results.

Mrs. Rosen sat up in bed reading a fashion magazine from a stack on the table next to pictures of her daughters posed in front of a white ranch house. A vase of roses balanced on the windowsill, and a begonia plant stood in the shelves behind her bed with three 'Get Well' cards and a dying balloon. Out the window, Mallory saw the distant tracery of the bridge to the south and the river below it. It was sunny, and it looked as if it was going to be what his father would have called 'a scorcher,' although the room was dim and cool.

Mallory walked in and sat down on the empty chair next to the bed, throwing his right arm over the chair back as if he had all day to chat. He tried to give the impression that he was at leisure to talk about anything and everything. At the same time he tried to keep his visits to three minutes per patient.

'Well, Mrs. Rosen, how are you doing today?' he said.

'I'm scared.' She had a pale, narrow face and a cloud of black hair. She flipped through the pages of the magazine and put it down. 'Wait, I have a list of questions for you.'

'Terrific.' Inwardly, Mallory cursed. These written lists of questions took too much time. First the patient had to find the list – Mrs. Rosen was right now groping helplessly in the drawer of her night table. Then they had to decipher each question, squinting to read their own illegible handwriting. It went faster if Mallory took the list from them and read it himself, but often they wouldn't relinquish it. This habit of writing down questions had been diagnosed as a secondary disease in the latest *New England Journal of Medicine:* 'La Maladie du Petits Papiers.' Sometimes the questions had already been answered by the resident – or they were so fundamental, so irrelevant, that Mallory could see they were just a way of talking out fear, of maintaining some kind of closer contact with him – the man who might save them. If *he* was a patient, Mallory often thought, he would have asked what his chances were, and he would have asked until he got an answer. He was surprised at how seldom this question came up. Now he took a deep breath and tried to relax as Mrs. Rosen asked the first question. Was it all right for her to drink?'

'There's no reason why you shouldn't have a glass of wine.'

'I know these are silly questions,' she apologized.

'If they're important to you, they're important to me,' Mallory said, reminding himself that this was true. He didn't like doctors who didn't listen to patients, and there were plenty of them. On the other hand, a guy like Riley who spent all his time with patients and didn't do his research was another kind of problem. Mallory had his methods for cutting time with a patient down to a minimum – using the fewest possible words, answering questions in the simplest way, never volunteering information – but he also tried to throw himself into caring for the patients who needed it. He sat on their beds, he held their shoulders and crooned reassurance. He tried to give them what they needed from him as a man as well as a doctor. At the same time he tried to stay detached. Getting involved with patients was death, not just for him, but for all the other patients.

The next visit was to Dan Connors, a thirty-year-old man with metastatic melanoma. Dan was a patient everyone on the floor had come to respect – he had put off coming into the hospital until he had ten years on the job, so that his wife and children would get a better pension plan. The melanoma started more than a year ago on his chest, but now it was everywhere in his body. Mallory had removed the gory, black masses of disease from his chest and back, but it reappeared. This morning Dan lay curled and silent under the sheet, clearly depressed. Lately it had become harder and harder for him to digest food – every meal was vomited back up with wrenching pain.

Mallory had promised Dan that he would go home by August and spend some of the summer with his children. Both Mallory and Dan knew that he was going to die, but somehow this promise that he would go home had become terribly important. Now Mallory leaned over the bed as if he could breath life into his patient, telling him that he would go home to his sons and sit down and eat a meal with them. Dan smiled, but hardly acknowledged the encouragement.

On his way from Dan Connors's to Jack Halbreak's bed, Mallory was accosted by Lucy Sanders, a patient who shuffled down the hall dragging her IV pole.

'Dr. Mallory, when can I go home?' she demanded. She was two days post-op; Mallory hadn't been able to remove the tumors which were slowly blocking her intestines.

'How do you feel?' he said. He reached out to take her pulse.

'You wanna hold hands?' Lucy Sanders asked. She was a short, feisty woman in her sixties. Looking at her, Mallory remembered the gray mass of tumor pressed against her duodenum, and the feel of her body under his hands.

'Don't you think I'm well enough to go home?' she said.

'I don't know, we'll have to see,' Mallory said, he smiled and patted her on the shoulder.

'But when can I go home?' She moved to block his way with the IV pole, the bottle of glucose swung as she maneuvered in front of him.

'Maybe in a few days, if your blood count is all right. We'll see, Lucy, now let me by.' Gently he pushed the pole aside and laid a farewell hand on her shoulder.

'How about tomorrow, could you tell the nurses?' Mallory stepped forward again, but this time his way was blocked by the plastic tubing connecting the pole to her wrist. The pole was on one side of the hall and she was on the other.

'How about the day after tomorrow?' she said.

'Let me by.' Mallory spoke louder now – the pole was in front of him again.

'Will you just give me a definite answer, Doctor?' This time Mallory slid the pole aside and walked by. He survived by speed. He stayed ahead of his doubts. He knew how sick Lucy Sanders was; he had known since he reached into her abdominal cavity and felt the tumor growing around her artery, and he didn't want to think about it.

· II ·

When Kate began to sell magazine articles, she wanted an office of her own – a place to go where no one else ever went. She didn't know why. There was no reason why she couldn't work at the dining-room table with David gone all day, but she hated clearing her work off the table every night to set it for dinner. Kate had started writing her articles out of boredom at first. A piece on the Chelsea Flower Show when she and David had been in England, a piece on Loomis, Weiss for the *Journal*. In the past two years, she had focused on writing about art, and she had a reputation as someone who could write about it in readable language. She didn't make any money though. The more prestigious the magazine, the less it seemed to pay. During this time she had heard that a room upstairs in their building was available, but at first, when she had approached David, he had protested. Why couldn't she work at home? he wanted to know. Finally she had given up trying to explain and just insisted that she had to have it.

The room was at the top of the building in a square, stucco addition on the roof, which had originally been built as maids' rooms. The plaster was peeling, the fire escape crossed one window, but there was wonderful light, and it was hers, and Kate happily furnished it with an old desk chair from college days, a cheap daybed, and a table. Out the window were views of the city at the edge of the skyline, granite and copper temples flanked by columns and urns on top of the fancy buildings on Park Avenue, square stone cupolas on her own block, and the water-stained wooden towers of the cistern beyond Third.

The building had changed dramatically since Kate and

David moved in. Prices had gone up ten times. The old people on fixed incomes had been replaced by successful young doctors and lawyers – glossy men with blonde wives and children dressed in chic toddler's fashions.

The place where the change was most apparent was in the rooms around Kate's office on the roof. At first, Kate had shared the spaces up there with a young couple named Harry and Samantha, and with a scrawny French woman who had been someone's maid in the days when they were maids' rooms.

Harry had a broad, handsome face and curly, brown hair. Samantha had grown up in Grosse Pointe on the lake and spoke in a loud, upper-class honk. She had inherited some money, but Harry had apparently drunk and gambled her money away. When it was gone, Harry and Samantha had moved from one of the big apartments downstairs into two former maids' rooms. The move had unhinged Samantha. There were often screaming fights between her and Madame Barthélemy with whom they shared an antique communal bathroom.

'Get away from me you old bat! Fuck! Piss!' Samantha would yell in her Grosse Pointe lockjaw, shaking her tangled hair and stamping a worn Gucci pump.

'You tramp, you feelthy hoore,' Madame Barthélemy would screech back. 'I see you wid de ozzer men, you come here wid de ozzer men!'

When Harry and Samantha finally moved out – her parents intervened, and they went to a large duplex off Central Park West – the little rooms were rebuilt into a cozy pied-à-terre with a roof garden and sold to a rich couple from Bedford Hills, who bought it so they could spend the night in town if they were too tired to drive home after the opera.

Madame Barthélemy had one suit, with a tight skirt above the knee and a matching pillbox hat. Each morning at nine she left the building, walked determinedly around the block, and came back. Indoors, she wore a blue cotton shift which looked as if it had been sewn together from cut-up sheets. Her principal occupation and obsession was cleaning. If anyone bumped against the wall of the hallway, Madame Barthélemy darted out to scrub away the invisible spot. Often she scrubbed so hard, with old rags and a foaming ammonia mixture, that she left a new spot on the wall.

Once a week she swabbed down the hallway, muttering to herself in a slurred mixture of English and French. The fumes would seep under Kate's office door, and she would have to open all the windows. At other times there would be a scraping noise outside the door, and Madame Barthélemy would be out there in her skimpy blue shift, cleaning the hall doorways, spread-eagled against each one in turn like a giant white spider. Kate had heard from the doorman that Madame Barthélemy lived on a small pension and that because of the building's noneviction policy she was able to rent her room for a token fee. Every now and then, on holidays, or when some random memory triggered her madness, Madame Barthélemy would lock herself in her room and scream. Her high, whiny voice, howling at the top of its register, easily penetrated the walls. On those days, after a while, Kate would take the elevator downstairs and work at the dining-room table.

· 12 ·

David and Kate stopped going to the theater a few years ago. They both agreed that Broadway plays were mostly disappointments. The opera was too long, repertory theater too unreliable, so instead they went to the ballet. David subscribed, year after year, as a kind of dutiful obeisance to the New York god of culture, and although Kate pretended to share his attitude, she had a secret passion for the ballet. The music and exquisite artificiality of the dances, the dancers' unearthly movements, thrilled her. Sometimes she just sat and daydreamed and couldn't remember afterward what she had seen. Sometimes she looked at the stage through David's binoculars, scrutinizing the ballerinas' makeup, their thin gold necklaces which were invisible from the orchestra, and noticing which ones were fatter, which prettier, and which had on costumes that had been hastily pinned together. With the binoculars she felt like an intruder, a prurient spy into a world which wasn't meant to be observed. Sometimes she just relaxed and let the glittering figures twirl.

But during the first dances of their last subscription of the season, Kate began to sink. She stared up at the golden loops of curtain above the stage, and the glimmering, faceted lights on the balconies, she took the binoculars and noticed that Heather Watts was wearing a tiny gold chain with one diamond at the throat and that Ib Andersen wasn't smiling as he danced Balanchine's opulent interpretation of Schumann. She thought about the pain of dancing, the blistered feet, the injuries, but nothing helped. In the darkness her fears began to well up inside her. She had an odd sense of dislocation, as if she were leading someone else's life – someone who lived a happy upper-class life on the Upper East Side with a nice husband. Cooped up in the theater, seated in the middle of a long row of strangers, she felt trapped, as if she were losing touch with whatever had kept her sane – whatever had enabled her to behave like other people all this time.

Finally the lights went up. 'Let's stretch our legs,' David said. The bustle and chatter of the lobby in the intermission dissipated Kate's disorientation. She and David chatted with a publisher they knew and a couple from the firm. Outside on the balcony they watched the fountain play in the plaza, the lights turning the water into fragments of jewels. David bought her a cup of coffee.

But after the intermission it was worse. The dance was The Goldberg Variations, and the spare, delicate piano music seemed to unlock her feelings. As the music developed into its beautifully complex theme and the dancers spun and jumped on the stage, Kate began to cry silently. Images of her mother, from the past and from the present when she kept insisting that nothing was wrong, flooded in on her. Her mother was a young beautiful woman in photographs with Kate's father, with all the world before them. Her mother standing in the kitchen, swearing at the broccoli. Her mother in the doctor's office. Her mother looking confused and waving goodbye as Kate was driven off to camp by another family, and the sharp, yearning pain that began once her mother was out of sight. Kate began crying harder. She remembered the warmth of her mother's arms, her childhood feeling that her mother could fix anything, could take care of anything – and her disappointment when that turned out not to be true. Sometime early in Kate's life, she and her mother had drawn back from their passionate need for each other and their passionate rivalry. Matilda Loomis had abdicated, leaving the field to her daughter who was left free to pursue her father with ardency and success which had made her father the most important man in her life. He still was, Kate thought, but he was dead. Her sobs escalated – the more she tried to suppress them the harder they shook her body. If she closed her mouth, they seemed to burst upward inside her, and when she opened it to breathe, wrenching, gasping noises mixed with the impeccable, sentient elegance of the music which had become more complicated in preparation for the final movements. The man sitting on Kate's right looked over and then looked away. Someone else's problem. But David looked straight ahead, staring up at the stage as if nothing was happening. How could he not notice? Kate could make whatever scene she wanted, his stance seemed to be telling her, but she shouldn't expect him to get involved in it.

'David?' she said in a whisper, as she drew in a breath between sobs. She reached out to touch his sleeve. The familiar feel of the summer jacket they had bought together calmed her, but he didn't turn. The sobs continued. David put a casual arm around her and patted her shoulder. The carelessness of the gesture infuriated her. She was in agony, and he patted her shoulder! Was it wrong to be upset? She couldn't help it. Was it wrong to weep for your dead father and your dying mother? Slowly the crying slowed and stopped, but Kate's resentment burned. The music was soft and simple now as the piece ended, the pianist's fingers whispering feelings to the keys. David would never understand her or the intensity of her feelings, Kate thought, and she might as well realize it. It would take someone more passionate, someone who was not frightened by feelings to understand her. She sat blank and dry-eyed as the last movement ended and the lights went up. The curtain came down, and David and the rest of the audience burst into enthusiastic applause. A stillness settled on Kate as the curtains were held open for the dancers to come out and take their bows. 'Bravo, bravo,' a man behind them shouted.

'God, Farrell was wonderful,' David said as they walked up Central Park West on their way home. Although they lived on the other side of the park, it was after dark, and they could no longer cross it safely. Instead they walked a while along it and then took a cab.

'How could you ignore me?' Kate asked. The stillness in the theater had passed and her indignation returned.

'What?' David said, he hadn't heard her.

'I said how could you ignore me? I was crying, didn't you see that I was crying?'

'I wasn't sure,' David said, 'I put my arm around you.'

'How could you sit next to me and not notice how upset I was?'

'I did notice.'

'Why didn't you do something?' Now they were walking past the Museum of Natural History. The building loomed over them like a brooding prehistoric animal.

'I didn't know what to do, I was afraid that I might just make it worse.'

'I think you were just afraid, period.'

'Maybe I was, you're pretty overwhelming sometimes, Kate, it's hard for me to know exactly the right thing to do. I do sympathize, Katie.'

'Well, it's harder for me, for Christ's sake. This is so typical! I'm the one who's upset, really upset, and now you're talking about how hard it is for you.'

'I didn't mean to do that.' David spoke softly and deliberately, as if he wasn't sure Kate could understand him. 'I know, or I try to know, how hard these things are for you.'

'You're trying and I'm crying,' she said. 'Ha, ha.'

'Kate, I know you're upset. I know you have a lot to be upset about, but please try to remember that what's happened to your mother and your father, that those things are not my fault. I want to help you, I'm on your side.'

'As long as I don't scare the horses.'

'That's unfair. You know, when people love each other, difficulties can bring them together instead of tearing them apart.'

'When people love each other,' Kate said.

David didn't answer.

· 13 ·

On the morning that Dr. Riley did call, Madame Barthélemy was having one of her shrieking fits. It was hard to tell why. The weather was balmy and New York's hundreds of scraps of garden, potted trees, and window boxes were blooming. The summer heat stirs up everyone's feelings, Kate thought, as the irregular bursts of human sound assaulted her eardrums. First she put in her earplugs, but the sound seemed to be more a vibration than a noise, and she continued to hear it through her nerves although her ears were blocked. Then she turned on the stereo, a Beethoven symphony, loud. This worked for a minute, but soon she heard Madame Barthélemy shuffle down the corridor, and pounding on her door was added to the screams. She turned the stereo down, and she was about to turn it off and go downstairs when the telephone rang.

'How is your mother doing?' he asked.

Kate dragged the telephone over to the door of her office and piled pillows from the daybed against it, hoping to block out the embarrassing din of madness. In the background, as Dr. Riley spoke, she could hear more melodic shrieks from his office radio. She recognized *La Traviata* – Violetta was singing. Gideon Loomis had loved Italian opera.

'She's okay,' Kate said, 'as well as can be expected. I made the appointments with Dr. Harris's secretary. My mother's just pretending that this isn't happening – that's her way of dealing with fear, I guess.'

'It's one method. Are *you* frightened?'

'Oh, I suppose so,' Kate said offhandedly, but the question surprised her. She hadn't really thought about her own feelings. 'It's not knowing what's going to happen,' she said slowly, thinking it out as she spoke. 'It's the uncertainty that scares me the most, I guess. I remember with my father that I almost wanted him to die sometimes, just so that the uncertainty would be over – I felt terrible about that.'

'That's a normal reaction,' Riley said, 'the uncertainty is the hardest thing. I've noticed that patients can deal with almost anything – even death – better than they can deal with not knowing. That's what really breaks people down. What's that funny noise?'

'My neighbor up here, I'm up in my office. She lives down the hall, and every now and then she goes a little nuts.'

'Does she bother you?'

'Not too much. It's so great to have my own place to work that it would take more than a little screaming to bother me.'

'You don't work at home?'

Now Alfredo was singing in a sweet tenor about his love for Violetta. Kate and her father had sat in the big living room in the house in Briarcliff, and listened to this aria, bound together by their separate experience of the music. Her mother's decorators had created a luxurious room, with draped silk curtains, deep oriental carpets, and cushioned chairs. Afternoon light streamed through the windows, taking on the blue and apricot shades of the silk. Her father drank brown whiskey from a crystal glass and stared into the fire. Through the pantry from the kitchen came the homey clinks and clunks of crockery and pots as her mother cooked.

'No, I have a little room of my own, it's in the same building as our apartment, on the top.'

'I'd like to see that sometime,' Dr. Riley said.

'It's not much, it's kind of a mess.' The table was piled with papers, things she had meant to read or sort through or file in the marked cardboard folders David had given her because he thought she should organize. The old stereo turntable jutted out beyond the shelf next to the daybed. The lamp was a bent leftover, and plaster was peeling and crumbling on the south wall where the roof of the building had a slow, apparently irreparable, leak. 'It's not at all like The Ascot,' she said.

'That's what I'm calling about, actually. I'm going to be over there tomorrow. Some workmen are coming, and some other people may drop by. Would you like to come about four?'

'Great,' Kate said. she didn't like the sound of other people dropping by. She had hoped that Dr. Riley would want to arrange things so that they would be alone together. Maybe afterward, when the other people had gone, he would ask her to stay.

Kate hung up, but her fantasy continued. She couldn't get Macklin Riley out of her mind – and she didn't want to. Why was she daydreaming about a man she hardly knew? The Ascot was an ugly, impersonal building which embodied all the greed and power of New York real estate developers. Why did it seem interesting and glamorous to buy an apartment there? And why was she so intent on Macklin Riley sexually? She was married, and he certainly wasn't particularly handsome. In fact, she couldn't even really remember what he looked like. He came from the strata of society that David always called 'the element.' Was it the power of his position at the hospital that attracted her? The contrast between the friendly way he treated her and the indifference and rudeness with which she and her father had been treated there two years before? Nothing else in the world seemed real except Dr. Macklin Riley and his soft, deep voice and his blue, blue eyes.

Kate spent the morning after his telephone call gazing out the windows of her office at the skyline and the water towers, and dreaming of making love to Macklin Riley on the parquet floor of his empty apartment, with the late afternoon sun coming in past the absurd little balcony outside the windows. It was tomorrow! He would meet her in the lobby, and they would ride up the elevator alone together.

'I thought I would take my clothes off,' she would say. 'Isn't that what doctors always ask you to do?' If only she could remember what he looked like! 'Yes,' he would say. 'Oh yes, yes, yes.'

· 14 ·

The entrance to The Ascot was on a side street in the east sixties, a few blocks south of the hospital. A boxy canopy with The Ascot written in gold script hung out over the front door, but the building didn't really need identification because it was impossible to miss. Its rounded, glass-and-metal facade appeared to have fallen from the sky and stuck in the ground like a glittering spear amid its shorter, drabber brownstone neighbors. The marble-floored lobby and chrome fittings reflected an idea of elegance relating to technology rather than architecture. Huge abstract paintings hung on the lobby walls, amalgams of a variety of abstract expressionist styles – shallow reflections of the paintings that were almost universally laughed at in the 1950s and now commanded million-dollar price tags, corporate respect, and critical reverence.

The broad entryway to the elevator bank was unfurnished, and Kate's footsteps echoed against the marble walls and floor. A poker-faced doorman ushered visitors in and over to a poker-faced concierge seated behind a long sweep of brass and slate, who gestured silently toward the elevator bank manned by a poker-faced operator. All wore blue and gold livery. The elevators made a slight swooshing sound as they descended and ascended, tracked by a row of lights in a pink marble panel.

Kate wondered who lived at The Ascot. Businessmen, she guessed, and people from out of town who were sick of hotel rooms, and very successful dentists. The building felt empty. There was no one else waiting for the elevators or in the hallway on the fifteenth floor. She walked down the hall past the closed doors of other apartments in eerie silence, leaving deep footprints on the dark green carpet, which gleamed under indirect lighting. It was like a hotel with no guests. Macklin Riley's door at the end of the hall was ajar, but Kate knocked anyway. Inside, she could hear voices and laughter, and then he appeared in the doorway, his bulky shoulders silhouetted against the light from big windows behind him. They shook hands. She couldn't see his face.

'Welcome,' he said, 'come in, what do you think?'

'This is lovely.' What else could she say? Kate stepped into the room. Behind Riley she saw a young woman standing, leaning slightly on one foot, in front of the windows at the opening of another door. She was wearing a navy suit with a high-necked white blouse. Kate's pants and sleeveless linen shirt seemed suddenly informal and girlish.

'This is Ann Lacey, Kate Weiss,' Riley said. Kate moved forward to shake hands, since that seemed to be expected. Was this cool female with the melodic name a real estate agent? Someone who had come to discuss decorating? One of the workmen Dr. Riley had mentioned when he invited Kate to drop by? Ann Lacey wore a discreet but elegant gold and diamond bar pin across the neck of her blouse, and a narrow matching bracelet.

'Kate is a writer,' Dr. Riley said, 'and Ann runs the family business.' His family business? What family business? Adrift and confused, Kate smiled. Dr. Riley acted as if this was all a matter of course, and she certainly didn't want to disappoint him. Her expectation that this Ann Lacey person would clear her throat, shake her petite head with its short, wavy brown hair, bat her big eyes one last time, and say that she had to be leaving now, began to fade as Macklin Riley showed them both around the empty apartment. There were two low-ceilinged, boxy rooms, joined by a tiny dark foyer. In the larger room, floor-to-ceiling windows gave an airplane-landing type of view of 62nd Street from Lexington Avenue to the East River and across to Queens.

Macklin Riley was wearing a blue blazer, tan pants, and a blue, oxford cloth shirt. To her relief, Kate saw that he was nice looking, if not exactly handsome. His face was long and looked drawn. This and his pockmarked skin gave him the manner of someone who had been through a terrible time and survived. The intensity of his blue eyes also seemed to be a reflection of internal struggles; he looked like a man who had been weathered by experience. As they walked around the apartment, he measured each wall with a tape, jotted the measurements on a prescription pad, and then transferred them to a precise architectural plan he had laid out on the floor. A worn, brown briefcase lay next to it with a doctor's beeper clipped to its edge.

As he measured and sketched, Ann and Kate drifted together in front of the huge, tinted double-paned windows. Kate imagined them as they must look, short and tall, trim and rangy, ladylike and girlish. Kate hoped that she wore privilege as gracefully and showed it as clearly as Ann Lacey. In the confined space of the living room, her limp was easy to hide.

Ann explained that she had grown up in the Bahamas – the way she described it as primitive made it clear that it was a luxurious family holding – but that her family had moved to Greenwich when she was twelve, and that she and her husband lived there too now. 'We live in Greenwich,' was what she said. She had left a job in management consulting to run the United States divisions of her family's business when her father had moved to Europe a few years ago. Ann spoke clearly and rapidly, in a girlish voice with the long vowels of the upper class. It was hard to imagine her serene, moneyed presence in the grubby confines of an office; she looked as if she belonged at the head of a boardroom table. Ann explained that she had had to be in town today for a business meeting at the Chase Manhattan Bank, and that she had come uptown to see Mack's new apartment and have a drink. She called him Mack in a breezy, proprietary way, and Kate wondered if she, Kate, was supposed to leave before they had their drink.

In spite of herself, she found she was trying to impress Ann Lacey, because she was impressed. Her heart-shaped face, too round to be really pretty, reminded Kate of the most successful girls at Langley Hall. Ann's body was made for field hockey and school uniforms, and her clothes looked fresh and pressed even on this steamy day. Was she Macklin Riley's friend, mistress, business associate? For a moment Kate wondered if he was trying to arrange a sexual threesome. The way Ann spoke to Riley, and the way he occasionally laid a hand on her shoulder, suggested an old intimacy. But he reached out to touch Kate's shoulder in the same way, and when he did, she felt a melting shock of warmth travel down from the point of contact to her feet.

As Riley finished his measuring and folded up the plans, the three of them walked to the other corner and stood in the glass angle of the two windows there, cantilevered out into space above the edge of Manhattan. The light was changing now, and in the street below them cabs and buses were backed up toward the Queensboro Bridge. Behind Riley's big shoulders, the gray apartment buildings across the East River on Roosevelt Island reflected the afternoon sun, while the lower roofs of Queens and Brooklyn already lay in shadow. Downriver, a great spout of water arched into the sky. Two wooden barges, nudged along by a red tugboat with a banded blue funnel, churned in the currents past Sutton Place. Behind Macklin Riley's ankles, knots of workers walked home uptown on Third Avenue. The height from which they watched, and the thick glass, made all this activity silent, as if the sound had been turned off in the world outside.

'Would you girls like to have a drink?' Riley stared out over the panorama of buildings and river. Although he turned toward them with a smile, Kate thought she saw sadness in his face and her heart warmed toward him.

'I don't have to hurry home,' Ann said. 'Scott's in Florida.'

'I'm okay,' Kate said. If they were out late, she would call David. Explaining that she was with Macklin Riley and his girlfriend would take care of any apprehensions he might have.

'Let's go have it at my old apartment. I'm packing to move and there's some decent wine there. I have something I want you both to see.'

'Your etchings?' Kate said. They all laughed.

· 15 ·

Macklin Riley's old apartment was a dingy studio on the tenth floor of a white-brick building on Third Avenue, near 79th Street. Three windows with metal frames looked out on sooty inner alleys and air shafts. The room was furnished with cheap chairs and a matching fold-out couch upholstered in the fabric that department stores call Haitian cotton. In one corner, a word processor sat on a Formica stand. Ann Lacey, cool and elegant, looked very out of place standing in front of the appliances in an indentation of the wall which passed for a kitchen. The shelves and cupboards were mostly empty. It looked as if no one lived there, except for one thing – the paintings on the wall. Five large pictures in lurid colors and hard splashy designs hung on every inch of space. The painter had obviously studied Color Field artists and then tried to improve on their method. The work combined the vagueness of abstraction with the sentimentality of greeting cards. As she walked from wall to wall, politely examining the congealed blobs of acrylic paint which alternated with a thin, uneven veneer, Kate saw that each one had a title typed on a card next to it – as if they were hanging in a gallery. *Manhattan Skyline* (three black blobs on a blue and brown background), *Rain in Paris* (a dozen blue drips on a red background), *For Mack* (an orange streak on a black background).

'What interesting paintings,' Ann said. Her voice sounded flat. Kate looked over, but her face was a blank. she wondered if Ann Lacey was dumber than she seemed, or just compulsively polite.

'Interesting,' she said.

'They are what I wanted to show you.' Macklin Riley swung his long arms around the room at the paintings. 'I've become something of an art collector. I don't have time to go to galleries and such, so when I got interested, I decided to concentrate on the work of one artist I liked.'

'Who is it?' Kate asked. She hoped her voice didn't betray her judgment. Dr. Riley was obviously so proud of himself for having acquired these abominable splashes!

'She's a wonderful woman. I don't know if you noticed, but the acrylic is baked on so they can be hung outdoors as well as in. She's in Paris now, but she's lived all over the world, in Africa and Russia, she speaks five languages, and she's had a really exciting artist's life. I met her in France, and one of the reasons I'm excited about the new apartment is that I think the work will look good there.'

Kate envisioned the cluttered, garish paintings on the bleak minimalist walls of The Ascot.

'It's odd how sometimes the most interesting people don't end up doing the most interesting work,' Ann Lacey said in a low voice. So she hated the paintings too! Their alliance of taste made Kate feel closer to her. Together they would educate Macklin Riley.

'It's true,' Kate said, 'often the best work is done by the worst people. Does this, what's-her-name, does she have a dealer in New York?'

'Mina, Mina Jonque,' Riley said as if reciting a sacred text — the artist's name. 'She's had a lot of shows all over the world, and I'm going to find her a dealer in New York.'

'I'm sure you will. There are hundreds of dealers now,' Kate said. And, she thought, millions of amateur artists trying to get those dealers to show them.

'I want her to have someone special.' For a moment Riley stared at the floor, then he laughed. 'You girls know a lot more about art than I do,' he said. 'I'm just trying to learn, do you think I've gone overboard? I really like Mina, if you met her you would too'.

'No one knows what makes good or bad art,' Kate said. 'It

really is a matter of taste more than judgment sometimes.' She sounded pompous; Riley's openness had thrilled her. He was flexible as well as strong. Even if he cared about something as much as he cared about these paintings, he was alert enough to pick up on other people's opinions and learn from them.

'I think maybe the *paintings* should go overboard,' Ann Lacey said in her cool, self-assured voice. They all laughed, but Kate saw that Riley caught Ann's eye and rewarded her for her honesty with a direct smile. She wished she had been more honest and less pedantic.

Behind the sofa the floor was crowded with twine and cardboard packing cases, the beginnings of a move. There were shopping bags overflowing with odd possessions; old sneakers, a brown blanket, a couple of dusty champagne corks saved from a long-ago celebration. Kate picked a leather album off the top of one of the boxes. Riley had disappeared around the corner into the kitchen alcove which was separated from the living room by white louvered doors.

'Hey, look at this,' Kate exclaimed, loudly enough for him to hear her. 'It's the Riley family album.' He stayed in the kitchen. Sitting together on the couch, Ann and Kate flipped through the first few pages of the book. The background of the photographs looked like a valley in Vermont or western Massachusetts. There was dirt instead of grass, and scrawny, second-growth trees. Two women, one wearing a flowered dress, and one who would have been pretty except for catalog clothes and teased black hair, sat on rocking chairs on a porch and grinned maniacally at the camera.

The porch was narrow with white posts and a wooden railing, and the paint was peeling. In another picture, the dark-haired woman sat bareback astride a big chestnut workhorse, in the background chickens pecked the dirt next to a ramshackle barn. In another, an older man, a gaunt version of Macklin Riley with white hair, leaned against a shiny new car. A shaggy, collie-type dog lay in the driveway next to one of the tires.

'We're discovering your family secrets,' Kate said when Riley reappeared, balancing three glasses of wine.

'Move over,' he settled himself between them. As he sat, Kate's attention moved below the album to where his hip and thigh were pressed against hers in the small space. When he shifted to open the book on his lap, his body rubbed against her. Was the same thing happening on the other side, where Ann Lacey was pressed against him? As Riley described each picture, turning through the plastic pages of the book, he seemed to become uncomfortable. She felt his body tighten and draw imperceptibly away.

'This is the house where my Aunt Netta lives, it's near us in Vermont,' he was saying, 'and this is my sister with a friend of my mother's.' He flipped more quickly through pages of the family in front of a Christmas tree. Kate caught a glimpse of a younger, darker, and much heavier Macklin Riley in a tuxedo, standing next to a tall girl in a wedding dress.

'Hey, let's see!' she said, but Riley had turned backward to another part of the book.

'These are the pictures I took with my first camera,' he said, and he seemed to relax again. Kate felt the heat of his thigh against hers as she stared at blurry pictures of rock collections, boats and trees. She could feel the warmth of contact with him the length of her nerves. Riley's poverty, the fact that he had come from a farm in rural New England, made him seem glamorous to her. He had decided what he wanted to be, and now he was busy achieving his dreams. He had created his own life instead of just accepting a life as she and David had. Gideon Loomis's idea of country was the country club – well-kept lawns, big trees, and maybe a tennis or a badminton court. Riley's country was something fierce and gritty and close to nature, a hard mysterious life which had left its traces on his character.

Now Riley turned to a section near the end of the album, a full-page photograph of his graduating class at the University of Vermont – five rows of undergraduates in robes and mortarboards, their youthful faces indistinct, almost featureless. As Riley's voice droned on, describing his graduation and the fate of some of his classmates, this one is a carpenter, that one moved to California, Kate noticed the shiny carapace and beady eyes of a cockroach sheltered in the binding of the album. She pressed herself away from Riley and against the arm of the sofa. Had Ann seen it? Did they have cockroaches in Greenwich, Connecticut?

'Excuse me a minute, girls,' Macklin Riley said. He closed the album and walked quickly into the hallway between the louvered doors of the kitchenette.

'It looks like an interesting place to grow up,' Ann said. Kate knew that she was being polite. The Riley farm looked like a rural slum. Loud banging noises came from the kitchen.

'Yes,' Kate agreed. She could match anyone's hypocrisy. 'I only know it from skiing, from Sugarbush.' The banging noises reached a crescendo.

'Have you ever been up there in the summer?' Ann asked. There was a huge crash from behind the louvered doors, and then silence. After a moment, Macklin Riley appeared without the album. He was smiling, but Kate thought he looked worried. Ann seemed completely oblivious to his tension and to the odd noises.

'Would anyone like another glass of wine?' he said. Kate remembered what an exterminator had once told her. For every cockroach you can see, there are fifty others hiding unseen in the walls and crevices of the apartment.

· 16 ·

Macklin Riley walked Kate and Ann out to the garage on Lexington where Ann had parked her car. It was a midsummer evening, and everyone they passed seemed to be holding hands or walking arm in arm. Although it wasn't dark yet, Kate felt a mysterious surge of freedom. She was alone, with new friends, people David didn't even know. For once, she wasn't part of a couple. For once, she wasn't with people who thought of her as half of David-and-Kate and never considered her separately. She had rarely been out at night without David since they were married. Anxiously, she felt in her purse for her keys and wallet – when she went out with David, he carried everything. She remembered with sharp nostalgia the joys of her brief single life – the image of herself as an adventuress. Once she had flown to California on a whim because she happened to be driving past the airport with a friend who wanted to go. She had driven with another girl from Spain up to London in a borrowed Morris Mini. She had gone home with an actor she picked up at the Frick museum. All that was over now. David had wanted to get married partly because he was afraid of the freedom of a single life. And she had been afraid to say no.

'Ann, you can drive Kate uptown,' Riley said as Ann's car, a deep green Mercedes, was driven out of the garage by an attendant. He gave them each a kiss on the cheek – as careful as a father to show equal affection for two daughters – and walked away as Ann put the car in gear and turned down the street.

Kate leaned back in the leather seat and stretched her legs forward toward the carpeted recesses of the Lacey car. Her family had always had Buicks or Dodges. The car smelled of leather and wax and moved quietly down the noisy street as if it floated just above the asphalt.

'Tell me everything you know about Macklin Riley,' Kate said, and she laughed lightly to show that this was a joke.

'He doesn't like cockroaches,' Ann said. They both giggled. 'But after what we said about those awful paintings, I didn't want to push it.'

'I wasn't sure you'd noticed.'

'Oh, I noticed, but I said to myself, Ann, give this guy a *break!*'

'He deserved it,' Kate said.

'Really, I don't know a lot about him. He came out to Greenwich for lunch once, very polite, I mean he ate with a fork and everything. I took him over to Port Chester to visit one of the factories. We make gelatin containers for pills over there, and he seemed interested. Which is your building?'

'This one.' It was getting dark, and men and women hurried up Lexington Avenue from work and swarmed out of the subway. The lights of the vegetable market down the street glowed through its green and white awning. The digital clock on the car's gleaming dashboard said 7:03 – Kate was relieved and disappointed. She wouldn't have to lie to David. Somehow the intensity of her attachment to Macklin Riley, and now to Ann Lacey, made her wish that she did have to lie.

'How did you meet him?' Kate asked. 'I have the impression he doesn't get out of the hospital much.'

'Oh, well,' now Ann seemed to hesitate. 'We sort of decided not to stress this with you, Mack thought it might seem odd, but you might as well know. We met him the same way, my mother is a patient of his. She's in for another treatment, in fact, that's why I came in today.'

'Your mother is at Parkinson?'

'Yes, breast cancer. Mack has been treating her for more than six months now.'

'And before?'

Ann shrugged. 'It's the same old story. She was out at Connecticut Hospital, and they kept saying there was nothing to worry about. They didn't catch it when they should have. I think Daddy's bringing suit against them. To me that's all water under the bridge; what's important is that we're doing the right treatments now.'

'Radiation? Chemo?'

'She's had all of that, everything Mack could think of, and even some experimental stuff that most of the doctors frown on.'

'She's had a second recurrence?'

'Yes, this time they took more lymph nodes, and they're saying it's all out, but you know, it's a waiting game. It could metastasize to the lungs, it could go to the abdomen, and there have been some symptoms.'

'What does Dr. Riley think?'

'He's hoping to try a new protocol and give her another course of treatment. If it were any other doctor, I think we'd say no.' Ann's voice was low and calm.

'Just like that. You'd say no?'

'You have to make these decisions, don't you think? At every step in these treatments, there's the possibility of refusing treatment.'

'You'd just take her home?'

'Sure, why not?'

It hadn't occurred to Kate that this was possible. That a patient's family could just take over the situation and make decisions for themselves. Ann seemed completely at home with this kind of power, this idea that doctors and hospitals were just people and institutions, 'I don't know,' she said, 'wouldn't you wonder, I mean if you'd done the right thing?'

'You always wonder when you make a hard decision, don't you? Does that keep you from making it?'

'I guess not. I'm not sure how my mother would react if we tried that.'

'I know my mother,' Ann said, but thinking of her mother seemed to shatter her cool manner and her voice broke. It occurred to Kate that she didn't really know her own mother, didn't know how she would respond if Kate decided she should refuse further treatment. 'She's magnificent,' Ann said now, speaking in a hoarser voice, 'I guess I never realized quite how magnificent.'

'That must be wonderful, to feel that way.' Kate didn't know what to say. She was impressed by Ann Lacey, by her authority and by her willingness to feel things. To the list of things that she half-envied about Ann, her money, her perfect hair, her delicate bones, her friendship with Riley, Kate now added her relationship with her mother.

'It was, it is,' Ann said. 'You know, above all, my mother's a fighter, I have the feeling she's not going to let this defeat her.'

'I think that makes a big difference, they say that attitude is a factor.'

'I tend to think that that's a way people have of reassuring themselves,' Ann said. Her voice was normal again. 'If attitude has something to do with it, they have some control over it – and of course they don't, really.'

Kate thought about her own mother. Soon the radiation treatments would start. If that didn't work, there would be more operations, chemotherapy, and maybe more chemotherapy if that didn't work. They would have to decide about continuing treatment. Ann's comments made Kate wonder if they should have refused treatment for her father, treatments which in the end didn't seem to have made any difference. Soon she might find herself telling people that her mother was a fighter, that she had the feeling that her mother wasn't going to let this defeat her – telling them in a definite, cheery voice like Ann's so that she sounded convincing enough to believe it herself, almost. Ann started the engine and released the emergency brake.

'Let's talk some more,' Kate said, 'there aren't that many people who want to talk about these things.' She was also anxious to find out more about Ann Lacey's friendship with Macklin Riley.

'Sure,' Ann said, 'call me.' She opened a leather wallet and handed Kate a business card. In the dim light from the dashboard Kate could see the blue lettering on heavy vellum.

'Thanks for the ride,' Kate said. She closed the car door, which shut with a luxurious clunk, and walked under the canopy of her building, past the potted fir trees and the doorman, as the big, green car with monogrammed doors slid away from the curb. She felt close to Ann and even closer to Macklin Riley. As she pressed the elevator button, she had a pang of jealous anxiety. What if Mack Riley was in love with all that no-nonsense talk, with all that power? She let herself into the apartment with her key, and David walked out of the study to greet her. He looked insubstantial and slightly unfamiliar for a moment. Then he kissed her lightly on one cheek and asked her what she wanted to do about dinner.

· 17 ·

'Dan's worse tonight,' the late-shift nurse told Dr. Mallory when he came on the floor. 'We're all pretty depressed about it.' Mallory opened the chart. Dan Connors, thirty-year-old male patient with metastatic melanoma. He flipped through the pages of blood test results, hematocrits, operation reports, and pathology lab reports to the current notes made by the nurses or doctors who visited the patient. 'Usually cheerful, talked about dying tonight,' 'Can't digest food, complains about pain,' 'Vomiting, more weight loss,' each note was scrawled in a different handwriting.

First on his list tonight was Rachel Rosen, the housewife with stomach cancer. Her operation had been successful and no further treatment was required. Mallory had told the nurses that they could send her home tomorrow.

Mrs. Rosen's room was still adorned with a limp balloon, a vase of roses, a begonia plant, and pictures of her daughters, but now the patient smiled broadly in welcome as Dr. Mallory entered. Her fear had been replaced with euphoria and gratitude – a familiar transformation for Mallory's surgery patients.

'Dr. Mallory, hello, thank you for coming,' she said, beaming up at him. Her husband, a heavy man in a business suit sat in a chair next to the bed.

'I don't know how we can ever thank you,' he said. 'You saved her life.'

'You remember my own doctor told me it was hopeless.' Now Rachel Rosen laughed merrily at this diagnosis.

'I remember,' Mallory said. In fact, the Rosen case had been a simple tumor resection. In his examination of her, he hadn't seen any other signs of disease. The chances of its recurring were small, and so no chemotherapy or radiation was necessary, although some doctors would argue that. Rachel Rosen's original doctor was just your garden-variety internist who looked on cancer as a death sentence.

'Well,' he said, 'you'll be going home tomorrow.'

'I'll never forget what you've done,' Rachel Rosen said. She looked pretty now, her face flushed with thanks for his skill, her eyes sparkling above some kind of frilly bed jacket.

'I wish my children could meet you, you're a great man.'

'Just doing my job,' Mallory said, but he swung out of the room feeling better.

Dan Connors was in a half sleep when Mallory leaned over his bed, but he came to and smiled wanly when he saw the doctor. Mallory put a hand down to touch Dan's bony shoulder.

'Not so great, hunh?' he asked. Dan nodded and abandoned the effort to smile.

'Listen, Dan, I'm going to do another operation on you,' Mallory said. 'We're not going to get you home this way.' Dan looked blankly up at him. 'I think I can clear this digestive problem up with a relatively simple procedure.

Dan grimaced slightly, then smiled to hide his reaction, but Mallory noticed some color returning to his face. It would be risky, but he could clear out the intestines once again, and it would be worth it. Patients responded to action.

'It's a simple procedure, but it's going to hurt you, and it's not going to hurt me. It will hurt me in my mind where I care about you, but it's your body, Dan. I want you to call on all your strength. This is the way we'll get you home,' Mallory said, leaning forward and talking gently. Dan nodded his assent.

'It will probably be in the next few weeks,' Mallory said. 'I'll talk to your wife, and I'll let you know exactly what's going to happen.' He stood up and smiled down at the gaunt face. Dan was going to die, but he wasn't going to die a minute sooner than he had to, if Mallory could do anything about it.

'I'm going to get you home by August,' he said, 'you're going to

drink that beer and play with your kids and sit out in the sun.'
But as he turned and left the room, Mallory felt exhausted. It took a lot; what he got from the grateful patients like Rachel Rosen, he needed double and triple for the patients like Dan. He headed for the stairwell and the pediatrics floor. The next name on his card was Eddie Gomez.

Looking into the room through the open door, Mallory saw that Eddie was asleep. The sheet was pulled up over his little kid's chest and shoulders, and his baseball cap hung from one of the bedposts. For a moment he reminded Mallory of Jamie asleep in his own room at home. He looked at his watch, it was after ten, Jamie would be sleeping now just like this.

Then he noticed that Mack Riley was sitting in a chair next to the bed. It was late, but there were certainly a lot of things Riley should be doing if he was going to be at work at all. He sat very still, and for a moment Mallory thought perhaps he was asleep too, but then he looked up and stood. Quickly he rested his hand on Eddie's shoulder, and then he joined Mallory at the door.

'He just fell asleep,' he said. 'They gave him the morphine. He seems a little better today.'

'That's good news,' Mallory said. 'But, Mack, he's not even your patient, for Christ's sake.' Mallory bit his tongue. He didn't want to confront Mack Riley, but he was tired, and the image of Dan Connors wasting away upstairs floated unbidden into his mind.

'Is it against the rules to care about someone who's not my patient?'

'Sorry, Mack, it's late.'

'That's odd, because I know it is against the rules to care *too much* about someone who *is* my patient.'

'That's another issue.'

'Maybe, maybe not.' The two men had walked the length of the corridor and now stood in front of the door to the stairs. Mallory wished he was inside and sprinting up to his own office. Riley's voice was cordial, but there was an undercurrent of anger at the rules, at the administration, at Mallory.

'You know as well as I do the risks of getting too involved with patients, with their families, with anyone who has anything to do with this bloody job,' Mallory said. 'We're all tempted and the wise ones resist.'

'And the honest ones?' Riley asked.

'I don't have to tell you what to do, Mack, by the way, nice work on Mrs. Ingalls's case,' and Mallory was through the door and charging up the stairs. Riley stood there while the metal slab slowly closed in his face, and then he turned and started for the elevator bank. Mallory was right, of course, Mallory was always right. But sitting next to Eddie while he fell asleep, sitting there so that the little boy would know that he wasn't alone, made Riley feel more worthwhile than all the grateful housewives in the world.

· 18 ·

Kate lounged on the sofa and drank coffee. The hum of the air conditioners almost put her to sleep. David had left, she had read the paper, it was time to go to work. She put her feet up and stared at the ceiling. She was too tired to work, too hungry to work. It was hard to work in the summer. Everyone else was on vacation. She thought about New Hampshire, the huge pines, the lawns slanting down toward the lake. David, on the raft. Their white legs entangled in the pale green water, and before that. Once, in a rage of possession over a toy boat, Kate had thrown a bucket at David. The moment when the metal struck the side of his little boy's fair head was like a photograph in her memory. He crumpled to the sand, eyes shut, mouth open and screaming, blood spurting from his blond scalp.

It was a deep cut – the edge of the tin children's bucket was as sharp as a blade. Kate's grandfather, who was a doctor, had been reading the newspaper in a chair on the deck of the boathouse. He and Kate's uncle Max, who was also a doctor, rushed over to David and worked together to plaster the cut. Max carried him up to the car, and they sped away, leaving Kate in her bathing suit and sandals standing at the edge of the driveway. Later, in the afternoon, David came back from the hospital with a bandage, and he was fine. No one blamed Kate except herself. The accident left a tiny scar over David's right brow, a stitch of skin on his smooth forehead which reminded Kate how frail he really was. Reminded her that a flash of her passionate nature could leave him crumpled in the sand, his face covered with blood.

There was a lot of fighting as they grew up. They fought over toys and over presents and then over bicycles and over who would drive to whose house, or who had told their parents what secret. She tried to remember when they had stopped fighting. Was it after the accident, or when they got married? Now they lived in polite, neutral harmony. There was so much at stake. Marriage is serious business under any circumstances, but marriage to the son of your father's closest friend, a man you have known your whole life, well, it's irrevocable. The telephone rang, interrupting her.

'I have a question to ask you,' her mother said.

'How are you feeling? I made the radiation appointments.'

'It's not about that.'

'Oh,' Kate sat down in David's reading chair and leaned her elbows on the table.

'Would you mind if I gave your father's desk to the Salvation Army's annual drive out here? No one's using it.'

Kate moaned a negative before she had time to consider. She didn't want to upset her mother. It was true that the desk, a mahogany slab with a burgundy leather top curling away from the wood, sat gathering dust in the upstairs study where her father had worked when he worked at home. Everything else was still there too. His reference and financial books, big red and green and gold volumes in the bookcases, his ledger paper and his blue leather date book and his stationery, his sharpened pencils in an old Harvard mug. The last entry in the date book was April 7, 1981, and in the months after her father died, the upstairs study had been thick with his presence. Now it was fading, out of that room and out of the house where he had lived, ebbing out of the material world as if there were a slow death by disappearance, which follows the fast death of the body.

Afterward, Matilda Loomis hadn't moved anything or packed anything away. His clothes hung unused in the closets. When Kate opened the crowded hall closet, his hat fell out from the shelf where it had been jammed in next to the flag which had been draped over his coffin. His acrid, familiar smell rolled off the clothes, and Kate quickly shut the closet door. But now, although the clothes and the objects were still there, the person had seemed to fade out of them until there was nothing left. A whiff of the past, a few ragged images. Now Kate could stand in the upstairs study and breathe in her father's smell and look at his books without crying, or sleep in her old room downstairs without thinking that her father was just outside the door, walking up and down the stairs, or pacing in the library as he used to do when she was at home.

Even the trees her father had planted along the driveway, so unsuccessfully that it was a family joke, had lost their scrawny look and seemed just ordinary. When Gideon Loomis had died, he left his body so suddenly that Kate still wondered where he had gone. Now he had left the rest.

'Sure, go ahead,' Kate said, because she knew she had to. 'There's no point keeping that stuff around.' Maybe giving away her father's possessions would finally liberate her mother, Kate thought as she silently mourned the battered old desk.

'I don't want to do anything that will make you uncomfortable, I mean if you wanted it or anything.'

'No, that's silly.' When her mother got sick, Kate had wondered if hanging on to the past wasn't part of it. Her mother had failed to start over, she had not had the energy to begin a new life. She was still mired in the old one. Dr. Riley had told her that he often had patients who had lost a wife or husband in the past two or three years.

The house and her mother's life had changed very little since her father's death. Before, she had spent most of her time in the kitchen even when people were visiting. Sometimes a particularly polite or feminist guest would insist on standing in the kitchen while Matilda went about the business of cooking and cleaning. If they offered to help, Matilda always said no, it would be easier if she did things herself. Usually the guest would wander sheepishly back into the living room toward the conversation and laughter that swirled around the host. It didn't seem odd as long as Gideon Loomis was alive for the activity to be in the big room in front of the fire while his wife hummed and cooked in the next room.

Now there was no reason for visitors to sit in the living room. Still, everyone did. The kitchen was a big room with skylights and a stone floor, but there was nowhere to sit, except two stiff, rush-backed chairs in the middle of the room between the pantry and the stove. Matilda Loomis was always moving from one appliance to another, and in those chairs, one was always in the way. If visitors to the kitchen tried to stand up, they were always in the way anyway.

Every now and then, when they were visiting, Kate would wander into the kitchen and ask if she could help. She wanted to be closer to her mother, although she knew that was impossible. Sometime, a long time ago, before Kate could even remember, it had become impossible. All she was left with was the longing, and the respectful, friendly politeness that she and her mother had always used for communication. When Kate asked, her mother would stop for a moment, stooped over the sink or the stove and let out a huge sigh, as if her daughter had just announced the end of the world, and as if that was no more or less than she expected.

'Oh no, dear,' she would say. 'There's really nothing you can do.'

· 19 ·

In early mornings, before the phone started to ring, Dr. Macklin Riley tried to work on research papers. The high-and low-dosage studies he was at work on no longer interested him. He knew how the results were going to come out, but to make the statistics for a paper, he had to continue the study for another year. Impatience with the way the labs were run irritated Riley. Everything had to be documented a thousand times. Sometimes he imagined some grateful donor giving him the money for his own lab, and the beautiful efficiency with which he might run it. Then he laughed at himself.

In the afternoon, he had clinic. Clinic was the bulk of his job, and it was what he liked best and least about working at Parkinson. It meant seeing thirty or forty patients in what was scheduled to be three hours but usually took five, seeing them under extreme pressure in the small examining offices sandwiched between the waiting-rooms downstairs. Clinic was organized for the convenience of the doctors. It began at one o'clock, and all patients were told that they had a one o'clock appointment. This way some patients inevitably waited four or five hours, but the doctor's time was always filled. This way, Riley often thought with frustration, the patients were often angry as well as frightened by the time he saw them. He had written endless memos to the administration about the clinic system, but they had had no effect. He was just another doctor, just another complaint. Macklin Riley hated looking out at those rows of desperate faces waiting for a moment with him. It made him feel helpless, as if the crowds of patients were his own retreating army – as if he were losing some important battle.

His patients' gratitude when he was able to help, and even when he wasn't, was what made the job possible. It had made Tammy furious. She claimed that he was spoiled by all that, that he expected to get that kind of attention all the time. She told him he had a doctor complex. What she didn't know was the price he paid for it. All the times he couldn't help.

He divided the clinic patients into three groups: those who were coming for the first time with cancers which responded well to chemotherapy; those who came for chemotherapy after surgery; and those for whom chemotherapy had essentially failed, now coming in for what the department called 'salvage therapy.' Those were the cases that kept him up nights. Often, he felt like telling them not to come. If they knew how small their chances were, he thought, they wouldn't. He wouldn't if it was his life – and death. But he didn't want to deny them hope, and so there were patients he was treating with chemicals that made them feel worse than the disease, treating them in a depressing situation with long waits and rude secretaries.

Ten years ago, when he had first come to Parkinson, Mack Riley had followed everyone's advice and made it an absolute rule not to get involved with patients. He had turned down all their invitations, although they were often attractive and he was often lonely. Instead he had dined with other doctors, who reinforced his feeling that the patients weren't quite real, that they weren't people that he had to care about the way he might care about family and friends.

He couldn't remember exactly when he had started to relax the rule, or when he had started to feel that he was more like some of his patients than his colleagues. Now he found that he needed his patients' admiration and gratitude more and more in order to continue. Even when a patient died, the family often regarded Riley with love and loyalty. They understood that he had done his best. He knew it wasn't his character they responded to, but rather the power and knowledge he seemed to have as a doctor at Parkinson. It didn't matter.

Today, the first three patients were easy. All were undergoing the CMF protocol, a combination of the drugs Cytoxan, methotrexate, and 5 F.U. The visits were pretreatment checkups before they went next door to have a blood test and then, if their white-cell count was all right, sat in the chair with the long arm that looked like a college student's desk chair and held out their arms for the needle.

'Everything going smoothly?' the pharmacist poked his head into Riley's office between patients. Riley nodded. 'Looks like you had a rough night, single man about town.'

'Doctors always have rough nights,' Riley said, and he laughed. The pharmacist leered and shut the door. Riley remembered that Tammy had flirted with him once. He wished she'd remarry quickly and get him out from under these absurd alimony payments. He had overextended himself to buy the apartment in The Ascot – the bank was partial to doctors – but soon he was going to run short. His base salary was supplemented by a commission system in which he was paid by the patient. He saw as many patients as he could, making it harder to find time for the research.

The door opened, and the nurse ushered in his fourth patient, Mrs. Goldman, a sixty-four-year-old woman from Detroit with a recurrence of breast cancer, which had been surgically removed three years earlier. She arrived with two pale, adolescent grandsons in her wake, one carried a parcel wrapped in silver paper and tied with shiny green ribbon.

'Manny, give that to Dr. Riley,' Mrs. Goldman ordered as she bustled into one of the chairs. Clearly she was a lady used to being obeyed. 'It's Irish soda bread,' she announced. 'You're Irish, I'm Jewish, but I can bake.'

Riley murmured a thank you and put the package on the nurse's cart which would go up to his office after clinic.

He had to tell Mrs. Goldman that she should have chemotherapy, and that he wanted to admit her to the hospital for treatment this afternoon. He could see that it wasn't going to be easy.

'Am I going to lose my hair?' that was always the first question. Mrs. Goldman had a dyed cap of blonde hair that looked like a hat.

'You may lose some of it,' Riley said.

'Will I lose all of it?'

'Probably, yes.'

'And nausea, vomiting?'

'You may have some nausea, but we have something that helps with that now. Each case is different.'

'Mouth sores?'

'Yes, you may have some.'

'Why didn't I have to have this before when I had the operation?' Her voice had gone from brassy to querulous. 'Why do I have to have it now?'

'Maybe you didn't need it,' Riley said. You should have had it though, he thought. You were in a lousy hospital. If they'd treated you then, maybe we wouldn't be here now.

'God, I went through this with my brother seven years ago,' Mrs. Goldman exclaimed. 'I'm frightened. It was terrible for him, oh, doctor, it was terrible.'

'It's different for each patient. It may not be the same for you.'

'Haven't you guys come up with something better by now?' Mrs. Goldman had started to cry. Tears rolled down her wrinkled, brown cheeks.

'C'mon grammaw, aaawww grammmma,' her grandsons murmured helplessly from behind her.

'Maybe I should just skip it,' she said, weeping. 'My hair, the throwing up, the misery, I remember with Al what it was like.'

'Mrs. Goldman, I can promise you that it won't be the same.' Macklin Riley stood up from behind the desk and leaned over Mrs. Goldman, who looked as if she might sit there and cry all afternoon. Thirty-six patients were waiting. There was a department conference at 4:30. He put a calming hand on her shoulder. His brown, tasseled loafer tapped against the linoleum floor. 'Your chances of getting better are much higher with this treatment.'

'But isn't there something else?' Now Mrs. Goldman, who had sailed into the office like a proud little ship, was crumpled and sobbing.

'I'll see what I can do,' Riley said. 'In any case, let's get you admitted, okay? We'll see what we can do, and we won't do anything without talking it over, okay?' Gently, he massaged her shoulder. It was 1:37.

'Okay, Doc,' she said. 'I'm sorry.'

'Don't worry. It's all right to be upset. Now remember what I said, and I'll see you tomorrow.' He opened the office door to indicate that the interview was over. He would check and see if Mrs. Goldman was estrogen receptor positive. There had been studies recently showing that with some breast cancers in postmenopausal women tamoxifen worked as well as the CMF treatment. If her tumor was small enough, and if her cells were healthy enough to accept the tamoxifen, she might be a candidate. If Mrs. Goldman felt that strongly about it, the chemotherapy might not be good for her anyway. He just didn't have the energy to fight these battles anymore, even if it was for the patients' own good. He ushered her out and called the name of the next patient.

· 20 ·

'I want to applaud you for setting up your mother's radiation appointments,' Dr. Riley was saying. Kate cradled the receiver between her shoulder and jaw and sipped her coffee. The remains of breakfast and the paper were spread over the dining-room table.

'Are you kidding? I wanted to get them over with,' she said. Riley had called a few minutes after David left for work.

'They'll be over with soon, you sound a little anxious.'

'I am, I mean, I know the chances are that she'll be all right, but do you think twenty-five treatments is the right number? Dr. Harris wasn't so reassuring. I wish you were a radiologist too, I mean, are you sure that he knows what he's talking about, what if she needs more?'

'Harris doesn't talk much, I know, but he's a very good doctor, and twenty-five treatments is the usual course for this, Kate. Your mother should do very well.'

'Are there going to be a lot of side effects? And what's this about some kind of implant this brachytherapy, she's supposed to be in the hospital for three days, what's that about?'

'There shouldn't be side effects, if there are any, they won't appear till near the end of the treatment. The radiation only takes a few seconds, it's just like getting an X-ray. There can be cumulative effect, the tissues swell and such, there might be some mild nausea – but it's nothing that should really bother your mother. I'd like her to take some progestins too.'

'What for?'

'Well, let me give you a little physiology lecture.' Kate imagined Dr. Riley leaning back in his chair, his rugged face, his clear blue eyes. 'In the normal menstrual cycle, estrogens build up the lining of the uterus – the endometrium – and progestins slough it off. Occasionally the cells that build up can become malignant, and if that's happening, the progestins encourage those cells to make a speedy exit.'

'It's so interesting!' Kate said. The logic of the disease fascinated her.

'Well, I think it's more interesting to people who have a reason to be interested, like you do.'

'Most people don't know anything about cancer, have you noticed that? A lot of people think it's catching.'

'They might not be entirely wrong,' Riley said.

'Are you kidding?'

'Well, partly, of course it's not like the common cold, but there are some statistics and some similarities. I remember when I first looked through the microscope at leukemia I was sure it was the same thing that we used to have with the farm chickens, and that was highly contagious. When a chicken came down with that we'd kill them all and burn the coops.'

'But it wasn't the same disease, it just looked like it.'

'True, but there may be a virus which has something to do with it. You know, women who marry men whose previous wives have had cervical cancer are much more likely to get cervical cancer than the average woman.'

'Do *you* think it's catching?'

'What I think is that we don't know. After all these years of study, we still don't know very much. We've learned a lot about how to treat cancer, but there are still mysteries.'

'Do you think it's genetic?' Kate asked.

'It's such a common disease that it's hard to tell. It's not unusual for two or three people in a family to have it – or for one person to have it twice.'

'Sometimes it seems like an epidemic.'

'It's not an epidemic, it's the way we live. Listen, at least seventy percent of all cancers could be prevented if people did what we're telling them to do, if they changed their lives.'

'Seventy percent? What do you mean?' Kate swallowed the last of her coffee, it was cold.

'We smoke and drink and eat a high-fat diet. We live in cities and have fewer children later in life. Kate, everyone knows that eighty-five percent of all respiratory cancers are caused by smoking. Eighty-five percent! But people go on smoking. Everyone knows that booze and cigarettes, processed food, breathing in automobile exhaust, they all increase the risk. Do people do anything about it – not much!'

'They need to be educated.' Kate had never heard Riley so vehement.

'They *are* educated, they just choose to ignore what they know. It's the same with everything, less than twenty percent of people in cars wear seat belts – and they *know!* People just live their lives without thinking about it, and then, by the time I see them . . .' Riley's diatribe slowed and stopped, as if he had used up his energy trying to inform the uninformable.

'What's that about having children late, what difference does that make?' Kate asked. She felt defensive. She was part of the recalcitrant public that Riley had railed against. She would have her children late, if at all.

'Yes, that's just one factor. Nuns have an unusually high rate of breast and ovarian cancers. Estrogen levels drop after you have a child, and high estrogen levels increase the risks. Ergo, having children late or not having them at all increases the risks.'

'Do you know how unusual it is to find a doctor who will talk like this?' Kate asked, pushing her own situation out of her mind and focusing on Dr. Riley. 'I've known a lot of doctors, and you're really exceptional.'

'Were some of the doctors you've known the ones who treated your leg?' he asked.

'Usually people don't notice my leg,' Kate said slowly.

'Doctors notice these things.'

'There was an accident, a car accident, a long time ago.'

'Where was it treated? Was it some kind of multiple fracture or what?'

'Phelps Memorial and Westchester Hospital and Columbia-Presbyterian and New York Hospital.' Kate hated to talk about her leg. She wished no one would notice it, it wasn't anyone else's business. But she was flattered that Riley had asked. In the background she could hear some kind of orchestral music on his office radio.

'So you really did the rounds,' he gave a low whistle. 'It must have been hard on you, just a kid.'

'Yeah, it was hard.' Kate felt like crying. Riley's concern shattered the breezy toughness with which she usually talked about the accident.

'I'm sorry, you don't like to talk about it.'

'No, it's that usually people don't ask.'

'How can they not ask? An accident like that really changes things.'

'That's true,' Kate said. 'How come you know so much?' In the background she could hear the telephone ringing and the voice of a secretary saying that Dr. Riley was on another line.

Riley laughed and didn't answer her question. 'I'm going to try and put together a collection of Mina Jonque's slides to take around to galleries next week,' he said. 'I'd love to have your help. You know a lot more about these things than I do.'

'That would be nice,' Kate said.

· 21 ·

Kate's father's family had all been lawyers. Her mother's family were all doctors. Her maternal grandfather, David Travis, had been the dean of Johns Hopkins and one of the great medical men of his generation, and thirteen of Kate's cousins were doctors. Orthopedic surgeons, radiologists, pediatricians, psychiatrists.

Grandpa Travis had been so prominent in the medical community that when anyone in the family got sick, his old colleagues and students would be called, and strings pulled and power played. Kate had gotten the best care in the world for her leg, because of Dr. Travis, just as doctors had flown in from all over the country after her uncle Max's son was hit by a car, and her mother had the best orthopedist in Boston flown to Nantucket after she severed her thumb tendons while shucking an oyster one summer afternoon.

By the time Gideon Loomis was diagnosed as having cancer of the kidney, years later, Grandpa Travis had been dead for a decade. All of a sudden, the Loomises didn't know anyone. The old connections had stretched or broken, the heads of surgery and the deans of medical schools who had known David Travis were dead or had retired. No one in the family even knew anyone who had anything to do with cancer treatment; no one had thought they might ever need to know anyone who did. Even the name for cancer doctors – oncologists – had a harsh, unfamiliar sound.

There had been other doctors too. Ten years after the accident, when she had only been married to David for a few years and thought she still loved him, her leg had acted up.

Each step caused a sharp needle of pain reaching down from her knee to her inner arch. Dr. Brennan had retired and gone to California by that time, but he recommended Dr. Ricardo Charles at New York Hospital.

It had been Dr. Charles who did the final operation on Kate's leg, an operation so clean and so successful that it almost seemed it hadn't happened – and there were times when Kate couldn't believe that the rest of it had happened either.

Dr. Charles's waiting-room had been decorated like an English country house library, and it was crowded with beautiful women, young ones with silky flags of blonde hair, and older ones with heavy gold earrings and neat suits. Kate had felt childish in her flowered cotton dress and with her hair parted in the center and loose around her shoulders next to these women, but when she was finally ushered by the chic nurse into Dr. Charles's office and saw him sitting there, smiling at her from behind his desk, she felt like herself again. There were pictures of him on the wall with a blonde wife and three children, and degrees from Johns Hopkins and Yale. Ricardo made Kate feel, even during that first consultation, and later on the operating table, that she was special, that he recognized in her a passion and an intelligence missing in his other, conventionally beautiful patients.

But it wasn't until after the operation, when she had gone into his office for a follow-up exam, that he had taken her in his arms as she pushed herself off the high, vinyl-padded table covered with stiff paper.

'You're so passionate, you're so physical,' he had said. 'I want you.' This avowal had completely conquered Kate. Later she imagined over and over that he had made love to her right there on the crackly paper while the next patient waited. All she thought of for days was Ricardo Charles, although it was a week before he called her and asked her to meet him at his New York apartment. He didn't even offer to take her out to lunch, but Kate found this lack of preliminaries thrilling, as if it were evidence of the strength of his passion.

'I'm going to fuck you,' he would say as they kissed in the

doorway and Kate's body melted toward him. 'I'm going to put my hard cock inside you.'

And she was always ready to drop everything, cancel appointments with editors, and dash downtown and take off her clothes and lie in the double bed in Ricardo Charles's pied-à-terre while he talked to her and made love to her.

'I want you to ride my cock,' he would say, and then, 'Now I'm going to come, I'm going to come inside you.' With Ricardo sex was quick and straightforward; he never had time for more than his own pleasure, but his verbal commentary was more exciting to Kate than any physical foreplay. With David, sex usually took place in dour, panting silence. Those words were never said. It wasn't nice to talk that way. But Ricardo's selfish pleasure in her body obsessed Kate. While their affair went on, although he called her about every two weeks, she could think about nothing but when they would be together in bed again. When David made love to her, she imagined he was Ricardo.

The affair with Ricardo ended as quickly as it had begun, and much more painfully. He just stopped calling. When Kate called him, his lines were busy, or his secretary told her he was out of the office or out of town. When they finally talked, he made gentle excuses, but it was clear from the pitch of his voice that in his mind they had had each other, and that was that. Nothing had ever been promised, although Kate had had her fantasies about Ricardo leaving his wife and children and asking her to leave David. Of course she knew that was impossible. All along she had sensed that she was one of many, many affairs in his life – and that had made it more exciting. But when it was over, it was over. The sharp pain of separation, the empty spaces in her mind where Ricardo had been, sent Kate reeling back into the heaven of married life. At least she wasn't one of these single girls who had been seduced and abandoned by a married man. She wasn't alone; at least she had someone.

· 22 ·

Before, when she had been there with Dr. Riley and Ann Lacey, she hadn't noticed how shabby it was. Now, on her way to meet Riley at his old apartment, Kate noticed the patched linoleum in the halls and the bare light bulbs hanging from the ceiling. She could smell onions frying, and the heavy aroma of cooking spices mingled with the floral perfume which she had splashed liberally behind her ears and on her wrists in the cab on the way over. The tinny sound of televisions came from behind closed metal doors. She knew that she and David would never have lived in a place like this, no matter how poor they were. They had been brought up to feel special, and everything they chose had to be special somehow. This building was ordinary as well as shabby. They would have found something with light or space or elaborate moldings – something unusual no matter how run down or uncomfortable it was.

The gloomy light and the sounds of teeming life, the smells of food were exotic and sensual. Like everything about Macklin Riley, they highlighted the inadequacies, the emptiness of her life with David. What a relief it would be not to be so special, to leave the cultured, rarified air of her world, and descend into the rich, mysterious, physical life of ordinary people. This was the real world, the world where people ate and loved and satisfied themselves and had children without thinking about it, as people had done for centuries.

David had a snobby theory that people could be defined by class no matter how much money they had. If they were poor, and forced to live without light and healthy food, and soft clothing, when they got some money, if they ever did, they would just buy more of what they already had. They wanted what they were used to – the comforting familiar. They would have larger dark, noisy apartments, and eat more macaroni and pizza, and fill their walk-in closets with polyester clothes.

If the rich lost their money, David said, the same thing happened in reverse. They would live in small apartments, but the space would be chosen for light and distinction. They would have fewer clothes, but they would be good clothes, old clothes. All this was very reassuring. What David meant was that he would always be special no matter what happened to his money – their money. David would see Dr. Riley as an example of his snobby theory. The Ascot was very expensive, but it was as boxy, as ordinary as his studio.

The door to Dr. Riley's apartment was ajar, and inside Kate heard a low, clacking noise. It was a steamy evening, the hallway has hot, and a blast of cooler air made her skin tingle as she pushed the door open. Dr. Riley was sitting with his back to the door in front of the eerie, greenish glow of a word processor screen. The melodious chants of opera came from a stereo perched on a sagging packing crate. As she walked up behind him, Kate saw that his black, silvery hair waved down over the collar of his blue shirt which stretched tight across his broad shoulders. If a man like that took her in his arms, they would enfold her and protect her. She looked over one of his shoulders, at the glowing, green letters on the screen. 'The Result of Randomized Prospective Testing of Chemotherpay and Hormonal Therapy in Postmenopausal Patients with Advanced Breast Cancer.'

Kate gently rested her chin on his shoulder. 'Hi,' she said. She could smell her own perfume. Had he known she was standing there?

'Sit down a minute.' He didn't turn to look at her but patted the chair next to his. Kate sat. The two chairs scraped against each other. In spite of the air-conditioning, the room was hot. She leaned over, and her body released the sweet smell of perfume.

'Damn!' Riley said. He still hadn't looked at her. He

backspaced and started the line again. Then, 'Oh, Christ!' another mistake.

'I give up, this paper was supposed to be finished yesterday, damn it!' Dr. Riley turned abruptly, but then he smiled as if he had just noticed that she was there. Kate was wearing a tight, pale blue blouse and a long, gauzy shirt which fell between her legs and above her knees where she had pulled it in the heat. Smiling, Dr. Riley let his eyes rest on her shoulders, her breasts, her waist, her legs, and then brought them back up to her own eyes.

'You look nice,' he said. His gaze seemed to generate an inner heat.

'Thanks.' Kate felt her body responding to him, she sat absolutely still. Beads of sweat glistened on his forehead, and the thick hair was damp at the edges.

'You look hot,' she said, reaching out to smooth his hair. He stood up quickly.

'Would you like a drink or something? I'm glad you could make it,' he said. 'I asked Ann to drop by too.'

'Sure, I mean if you are.' Chagrin made Kate blush and stammer, she felt cold in the hot, heavy air. After her lies to David and all her worries, she was about to spend a chaste evening with another couple.

'She can't make it though, she's tied up with that jock husband of hers. She said she'd call later.'

'So I have you to myself?'

'I really should work, but let's have a drink at least. I wanted your help selecting Mina's slides, but who knows when I'll ever have time to do that.'

'Is Ann okay?' Damn Ann and damn Riley's work. Kate had imagined a long, romantic and consequential evening with Riley. Now he showed signs of kicking her out so that he could return to his beloved medical papers.

'She's fine, her mother . . . that woman is a class act,' he said enthusiastically. 'I've sent her home this week, but I'm afraid she'll be back before the summer's over. She'd rather be at home if she can be though, I can sympathize, she has a lovely home.'

'Is she better?'

Instead of answering, Riley turned back to the machine and pressed a series of keys. It hummed for a moment and then, with an earsplitting wheeze, the printer began to spit out a long sheet of paper.

'How come you're writing?' Kate asked. 'I'm the writer.'

'Research is a big part of my job, that's one reason I write papers.' Riley laughed. 'The other is that, if I don't, I get fired.'

'And the patients?'

'There's a lot less emphasis on that these days. Cancer isn't going to be cured by taking care of sick people; everyone's figured that out. It's going to be cured in someone's lab or research project.'

'But you're so good with patients! A lot of the doctors are terrible.'

'I always seem to be good at what's not required.' Riley laughed again and sat down, stretching an arm over the back of her chair.

'Do you think they're going to cure cancer?' Kate sat up straighter, pressing her shoulders up toward his arm.

'Jesus, Katie, I'm just trying to stay out of trouble, I can't answer a question like that.'

'Well, has there been progress, I mean since you started?'

'Sure, oh sure, when I first came, my first rotation at Parkinson, our introductory lecture was on an operation called the hemicorporectomy. What they did was, it was one of the great pioneer surgeon's ideas, they actually cut a person in half. I mean if the disease had metastasized to the thighbones and through the abdomen, they just cut off the bottom half. We don't do things like that any more.'

'Grisly,' Kate said. 'I think I'd rather give up.'

'That's what you say now, but people would almost rather do anything than give up. At least that's my observation. We have a few patients who are basically talking heads. Nothing's really working but the brain, but that's better than nothing at all.'

'I love hearing all this.'

'You do now, Kate, because of your mother. Doctors are just as boring as other people.'

'God, I don't think so. It's sort of heroic what you do – particularly when you look at the rest of the world. You don't make a lot of money, and you work those long hours under incredible stress, and it's all because you think you might help someone. I know, it sounds a little sappy, but . . .'

'I don't believe in heroism, I guess. People are born the way they are, they do what they do.' Riley let his arm rest across her shoulders; his hand lay close to her neck, touching her hair. Waves of sexual current swept down through her body from his touch.

'How can you say that! People change.'

'Do you really think so?' Riley slumped back, breaking contact with her, and looked into her eyes. He seemed terribly interested in her answer, as if whether or not she thought people changed was very, very important to him. His eyes gazed straight into hers as if there was nothing else in the room; she felt herself blushing.

'Yes, they do change. I've changed, having my father die, having my mother get sick, those things changed me.'

'And your leg?'

'Yes, I guess the accident changed me.'

'The circumstances changed, but do you think that you, the essential Kate, has changed?'

'I think so, circumstances create change, sure.' As she spoke, Kate looked at the floor and then back up into his eyes which were fixed on her like an embrace. They were inches apart, she felt drawn toward him as if his body was magnetized. 'I don't feel safe the way I used to, for instance. I used to think I was immune to disaster. I never wanted to know about cancer before because I knew I wasn't going to get it, no one I knew was going to get it. Now I do want to know.'

Riley leaned back away from her and smiled. 'Maybe you're just becoming a realist,' he said.

'But that's a change then.' She felt breathless, she could hear her pulse, her heart pounding in her chest.

'Not really, it's just that you're seeing things more clearly.' He laughed now and she laughed with him. 'You know the thing about you, Kate,' he said, 'is that you're really fun to talk to.'

'Hasn't this job changed you?' she asked, but his compliment made her blush again. The heat in the room increased her body's heat, she felt her hair damp against her forehead, a bead of sweat rolled slowly down her back.

'Oh, maybe.' He got up from his chair and slowly crossed the room, settling on the sofa with a sigh. Above him one of the paintings glowed in lurid red and black. There were paler patches on the wall where the others had been; Kate wondered if they had been sold. The last light of evening faded through the metal casement windows. 'I don't know, there are days when I think this job has changed me for the worse.' Riley's shirt was open, his skin looked damp with sweat.

'What do you mean?'

'It's almost unbearable sometimes, the helplessness I feel, having to watch people get sicker, and there's nothing I can do for them. Sometimes I don't know how other doctors go on performing.'

'Maybe they don't care about their patients as much as you do.'

'That's what they would say. I'm suffering from what is known as failure to sufficiently detach. That's even more depressing – if being a good doctor means not caring so much about your patients.'

'Think about all the people you help. Look what medicine has done in fifty years, come on! In fifteen years, even.'

'I guess so,' he said.

'You guess so?' Now Kate shifted around in her chair so that her body was facing him. 'What about antibiotics? People used to die of pneumonia, tuberculosis, diphtheria, are you kidding?' She uncrossed her legs, and opened her thighs so that her skirt fell between them. One hand rested on her inner thigh.

'You're so passionate,' he said, leaning back against the sofa, 'so passionate in other people's defense.'

'It's something to be passionate about.'

'What about you, what about your leg? There have been great advances made in orthopedics too.'

'What about it?'

'Didn't you tell me it was a car accident? It must have been some kind of multiple facture, what happened exactly?'

'Didn't we talk about this already?'

'How old were you, did you tell me?'

'Fifteen, it was in the car, with my father.' Her father was dead, the car a crumpled wreck.

'Come over here,' he said, 'can I have a look at it?' Kate crossed the room to the sofa which stood against the wall outside the circle of light from track lighting on the ceiling. Outdoors night had fallen. Piano music came from the stereo speaker and floated toward the shadowy walls. She sat down beside Riley, slipped off her sandals and raised her skirt above her knees.

'Come here,' he said, gently lifting her leg over his so that the injured knee was propped against his thighs and the other leg tucked under her against the cushions. His hands palpated the skin and seemed to burn as he moved them tenderly across the knee. Kate's nerves loosened, she relaxed against him.

'Wow,' he said softly as he felt the bones under the scarred flesh. 'It's amazing that you do as well as you do, it must have been touch and go with this leg.'

'They told me I'd never walk again,' Kate said. She tried to summon up her old indignation, but the past seemed blurred and distant. This sofa, Riley's hands on her flesh were the whole world.

'Well, they weren't entirely crazy, someone has done a lot of work here. None of the muscles in your leg are working normally. Wouldn't you like to get this fixed?'

'I already told you, no,' Kate said, her voice was level, but she felt dreamy, buoyant. Riley's hands seemed to be drawing her toward him.

'Sorry, I didn't mean to get you hot under the collar.' Now his hands rested on her legs above the knee with the skirt bunched against them, he was breathing harder, his mouth slightly open.

'I am *so* hot,' Kate said. She leaned forward, and he turned to meet her, opening his mouth against hers and sliding his tongue back and forth between her lips. For a moment, he tried to draw back.

'Kate,' he said, but she kissed him again, and this time he thrust his tongue deep into her, and his hands drew her toward him touching her breasts. He couldn't resist her; she could feel the heat of his desire. Deliberately, he put his hands on her waist and shifted her body toward him so that she was straddling his legs, kneeling on the sofa cushions. He began stroking her legs from the soles of her feet up to her thighs, going higher with each stroke. Kissing her again, with his tongue deep inside her, he pressed her body down against his. She could feel his erection pressing up against her between her legs. Only a thin layer of cloth separated them. His hands were on her everywhere now, brushing against her thighs, her breasts, pulling back her hair. Kate reached up to unbutton her shirt. But suddenly Riley drew away from her and inhaled deeply. Then he exhaled loudly, taking his hands off her body and laying them back on the sofa.

'Kate, Katie, we can't do this, I can't let this happen.' His voice was a hoarse whisper.

'You want it to happen.'

'I do, I do, but it's not . . . it can't happen.'

'Why not? Kate slid off and curled next to him. His body had suddenly gone cold, as if an electrical current had been turned off. His breathing was slower.

'It's not a good idea, not for you, not for me, not for a lot of reasons.'

'We're consenting adults, we're attracted to each other, why would we be hurting anyone?'

'It's you that I'm worried about, you're married, and there are a lot of reasons why it's not a good idea for doctors to get involved with their patients.'

'I'm not a patient.'

'You know what I mean, I'm sorry, I shouldn't have let it go so far, I behaved irresponsibly.'

'I like to feel that I'm responsible for myself,' Kate said. 'I think what happens to me is my own business.'

'Please don't be angry with me. It would be terrible if this stopped our being friends.' He seemed to be pleading with her. Kate shrugged, but she smiled.

'Good, let's get something to eat at least,' and Riley was up off the sofa and into the grimy kitchen. He emerged with a bottle of wine and a box of crackers.

Kate rearranged her skirt. All at once she remembered the cockroach, and she quickly put on her shoes. The telephone rang on the other side of the room.

'Oh Christ, why isn't the service picking up?' Riley put the wine down on the floor unopened and stepped over a packing crate to pick up the receiver.

'Oh, hi.' His reluctance to be interrupted turned to friendliness when he heard the voice at the other end of the wire. 'We were just talking about you a few minutes ago,' he said. 'Listen, there are some things I want to go over with you, let me call you back in about ten minutes, all right, will you be there?'

Kate stood up and straightened her clothes. She mustn't act disappointed. Riley turned to her.

'That's a good example of what I don't like about this job,' he said. 'I have to call Ann back and tell her some things about her mother that she doesn't want to hear. I'd much rather sit around and talk with you.' Kate was elated as Riley ushered her out of the apartment and kissed her good night, drawing her toward him for a moment.

'Mmmmm, you are so attractive,' he said, but when she slid her arms around him, he laughed and stepped back. She walked out of the building and up Third Avenue feeling good. Riley's involvement with Ann was about her mother, his involvement with Kate was about Kate. His feelings for her were so strong that he had been swept away in spite of his better judgment. He couldn't control himself. It was just a matter of time.

· 23 ·

Peter Mallory always knew when he was working too hard, because he would have the dream. In the dream, he would be doing rounds late at night. He entered a patient's room, and the patient looked up at him with pleading, helpless eyes. It would be his mother, in the dream, or Jane or little Jamie. When that happened, he tried to slow down, get a little more sleep, and work fewer seven-day stretches.

Friday was often a bad day in Mallory's clinic. He was tired, eyes sore and voice giving out after a string of seventeen-hour days, three trips back and forth to home in New Jersey, nine operations. As he saw patients, he usually got a second wind. The first was a young girl who was snappish because she had had to wait an hour. She had swollen glands and some blood imbalances, and Mallory told her that he couldn't help her. She should wait and see the endocrinologist. The girl shook her dark hair, moaned and hissed through her teeth. She had already waited an hour. Mallory apologized.

The next patient was upset because she hadn't been able to reach him on the telephone. She had left five messages, she complained. He questioned her closely. The idea that he might not be getting his messages was disturbing. He would have to call a staff meeting. The woman needed a second round of chemotherapy treatment. Problems.

'It's a full moon,' Mallory said to the nurse as he tossed a chart back on the secretary's desk. The next patient was a muscular twenty-three-year-old man who looked as if his principal thinking process was in distinguishing his lats from his pecs. A bodybuilder. He was chewing gum, and the sweet, synthetic smell bothered Mallory's nose. On the muscle man's thigh, a lump as big as a baby's fist protruded through the tanned skin. He was jumpy and scared, and he explained to Mallory that he had a buddy dying of lymphoma over at Lenox Hill. Mallory saw this a lot. The cancer wasn't contagious, but the fear was highly contagious. If it could happen to someone they knew, people realized, it could happen to them. Patients often brought in their children or wives with symptoms. The families of cancer patients were forced to realize that cancer is a random, arbitrary, and very common disease.

Mallory told the jock that the lump on his thigh looked benign, but that he should have it removed anyway. The guy cracked his gum.

Mallory hadn't eaten yet, and in between patients, he trotted down to the cafeteria. The surgeons ate in a windowless room at small Formica tables, on molded plastic chairs. Food came from a steam table against one wall; gluey soup, oozing sandwiches in cellophane, lots of muffins and brownies. Mallory unwrapped a muffin; the paper was oily and the heavy dough studded with chocolate chips. He picked up his sixth cup of coffee of the day and headed back up to the clinic.

Because of this break, Mallory had forgotten the Lanza family, who had been waiting for him in the examining room. 'Jesus,' Mallory hissed as he realized this. He gulped the last of the muffin and prepared to apologize, but the Lanzas didn't seem to mind. The old woman and her two sons sat patiently on their chairs. She had the wrinkled face and body of a field worker, but the sons had prospered – her neck was looped with gold chains and her head covered with a silk scarf.

The Lanza brothers' mother had stomach cancer. Mallory traced the gray mass on the CAT scan. He tried to explain this to her, and she nodded and smiled happily, not understanding a word. When he said he would like to operate next week, one of the brothers began to weep, sniveling into a monogrammed linen handkerchief. His mother reached out a brown hand to comfort him. The pretty nurse grimaced at Mallory as he headed out of the examining room and on to the next.

'It's the full moon,' she said.

Mallory felt as if he were pushing himself beyond limit, after limit. He'd been up since 4:30. His body moved slowly, occasionally he stumbled into a door frame, and once at about noon he fell off the doctor's stool. When he sat down to talk with a patient, he stayed a little longer to conserve his energy – to put off the job of getting back on his feet. Mallory was forty-five, but he looked older and seemed much older than that. Experience had completely matured him. All the emotional baby fat had been burned right off. There was no time for brooding or for questions. He wasn't thinking about his life, he wasn't planning his life, he was living his life, and it took all the energy he had.

After everyone else went home, or off to the country for the weekend, Mallory made his Friday night calls in his empty office. The secretaries had left hours ago, leaving stacks of messages on his desk. Sometimes they had copied down the numbers wrong, and Mallory had to call and recall, or look up the number himself. He did it. He called the family of a young girl with multiple melanomas. She had slipped into a coma.

'Well, my friend, I think you're nearing the end of the road,' he said to her father. He sounded friendly and sad. This was a girl he had come to know pretty well in the two years he had treated her. He tapped out the next number, the daughter of a man whose tumor had turned out to be inoperable in the OR this morning.

'The chances of him having a remission are low,' he said. 'I couldn't touch the tumor; it's too close to the aorta. I don't know how long it will be, but I think we can send him home next week.' After that he called Dan Connor's wife to talk about the operation he was going to perform on Dan, Monday morning. She said she would be waiting for news in the patients' lounge at about noon. Then he called the father of a teenager with stomach cancer. The operation hadn't worked. The disease had recurred in the boy's lungs. Mallory remembered the way the kid had looked today in his hospital gown and basketball socks.

'A cure in this case would be a miracle,' he said into the

telephone. 'I think he will deal with this situation with denial, and that's fine. If he asks any questions and you don't know what to say, just have him call me.'

Outside the office window, he could see the lights of Queens across the East River. It was after eight now. The traffic jams of people on the way to the country would be thinning out in the midtown tunnel and on the Long Island Expressway. The restaurants along Third Avenue were filling up while he talked. Jane would be pissed off when he got home. Across from his desk was the sofa and guest book, on his walls degrees and photographs of men he had worked with. Most of what he said on the telephone was reassurance. Not that the patient would live – but that the survivors would somehow survive. He called everyone back. The doctors who had called him during the day had gone home, and he left messages for them. The patients and their families were always there after the first ring or two, waiting for his call.

Mallory looked up as someone passed from the bright lights of the hall into the shadows of the anteroom coming toward his office. He was surprised to see Macklin Riley, standing framed in his doorway.

'Riley! Working late?'

'Just wandering.' Riley looked tired. Mallory remembered he was recently separated from his wife. He probably had nowhere to go.

'These late-night phone calls,' Mallory complained, 'come on in and listen. I'm a goddamned psychiatrist.'

Riley laughed. 'I could probably use that,' he said.

'Have you dropped in on Eddie? How's he feeling?'

'His white-cell count seems to have stabilized,' Riley said. He sat heavily down on the sofa, Mallory wanted to be friendly, but he hoped Riley wasn't settling in for a long chat. He *did* have somewhere to go, and he was already pretty late.

'That's a Harvard answer,' Mallory said.

Riley smiled. 'I remember. It's correct but it doesn't answer the question. Okay, Eddie's feeling lousy. I think his denial is fraying; it's getting to him, and his mother's a goddamn wreck.

It's terrible for her, so terrible that she can't spare him. If we could keep these kids away from their nearest and dearest, they'd be a lot better off.' Riley wondered what it would be like to have a son, a son who was dying. Would he be strong enough to spare the boy, strong enough to survive?

'But we can't.' Mallory pulled a stack of letters toward him over the desk and began to sign them as he talked.

'Yeah, there's a lot we can't do,' Riley hoisted himself off the sofa and ambled toward the door. He moved as slowly as Mallory moved fast.

'Good night, Mack,' Mallory said, but he was gone, through the shadows and around the corner of the hallway.

Mallory sipped his coffee and pushed his telephone buttons, signing more of the letters with his free hand.

'Yes, sir,' this time he was speaking to a patient with renal cancer, the man was angry. 'Well, sir, I'm afraid that on the X-rays you do have metastases to the lungs. Yes, I do think the disease has spread. I'm sorry, there's no easy way to tell you that.' His voice was ragged by now. Another man would have asked himself why Riley had dropped in, or wondered if he was dealing correctly with the problem of the younger doctor. Peter Mallory didn't waste time with questions like that. He finished signing the pile of letters as he tapped out the next number. Dinner and bed were hours away.

'It depends on the pathology,' he told a woman whose mother would be operated on Monday. 'Yes, I will be doing the operation, and I certainly hope to remove the tumor. I have assistants, but I will be doing the operation myself.' Mallory thought of the OR with its odd light and the smells of burnt flesh and the iron smell of blood. The clamps, the suction, and the way he dropped stitches from his fingers into the tissue in a neat, perfect row. The body wasn't perfect so his work had to be. Yes, he had assistants. Yesterday, the resident had clamped off the wrong blood vessel. If he hadn't been there . . . 'I'll be there,' he told the woman.

Above Mallory's head, on the wall, was one of Jamie's crayon drawings. He thought about Jamie's room at home. His clown wallpaper and the fire-engine box of toys. The baseball and basketball paraphernalia and the brand-new bicycle. The little boy might even be asleep by now.

'We'll just have to take care of it as best we can,' he was saying to a woman whose husband had pancreatic cancer. 'What we're talking about here is buying time.'

· 24 ·

'How are you feeling?' Kate asked her mother. The morning light streamed into the bedroom of the apartment onto the pillows of the unmade bed. It was hot, one of the killer days of summer, and she had turned the air conditioners on full blast. The roar made it difficult to hear her mother's high, slight voice through the receiver.

'I wish everyone would stop asking me that. I'm fine,' Matilda Loomis said, as if her definiteness could make that true. 'There's nothing wrong with me.'

'No more stomachaches.'

'Don't be a worrywart, that was just those shrimps I had at Tino's.'

'Your head's okay?'

'I never had headaches.'

'That's not what I meant.'

'Don't worry about me,' her mother said with a long sigh.

'Mom, I can't help worrying about you. We're all worried. In a way I think it will be easier when these treatments have started.'

'Don't be ridiculous.'

'Do you have an appointment with Dr. Riley before you see Dr. Harris?'

'Oh, I don't know.' Her mother's voice registered exasperation now. 'I can't keep all these doctors straight. It's too hot to go into the city anyway. It's so humid out here, the lawns are burning up and my flower beds are in trouble. I don't know how the vegetable garden is going to survive.'

'Well, listen, I'm going to come out and take you to your first appointment, okay?'

'Oh, Kate you don't have to do that.'

'I know I don't have to. I want to.'

'Did I tell you that Don Anderson took me to Elsie Spetter's for dinner last week and I sat next to the nicest doctor who used to be at Parkinson Hospital. He's a friend of Don's from somewhere.'

Don Anderson was a widower who lived over the hill from her mother's house. Gideon Loomis had never liked him, so Kate didn't know him well.

'His name is Harold Baker, Dr. Baker,' her mother continued, 'and he said that Parkinson Hospital is a terrible place and I should try to avoid going there. Elsie said the same thing, she said no one knows if cancer is contagious, and a hospital like that that treats only cancer . . .'

'It's been arranged so that you probably won't have to go, but if you did have to I think it's the best . . .'

'Remember what they did to your father!'

'They did what they could, it was the disease that did that, Mom, not the hospital. And as for being contagious, you know that's ridiculous.'

'How do you know it's ridiculous? First your father had it, and now I have it,' her mother's voice broke.

'You're frightened, Mom,' Kate said. 'Don't let people get to you that way. Everyone has their own cancer horror stories, remember when Dad had it the things people told us? You can't listen.'

'Dr. Baker said they used to have a surgeon at Parkinson called the butcher, he said this surgeon used to cut people in half!'

'I'm sure that doesn't happen,' Kate said. She remembered Riley's lighthearted description of the hemicorporectomy and decided not to try and explain it to her mother.

'And he said it was a teaching hospital, and they use their patients for their experiments. He said they don't even care how they treat the patients, all they care about is their research. They use patients just to get material for the papers they write.'

'Just because they're interested in research doesn't mean

they're not interested in patients,' Kate said. 'Some of the doctors there are cold and awful, but Dr. Riley is really nice, he does care.' She wanted to kill Dr. Harold Baker, whoever he was.

'Of course he's nice to you. You're young and pretty, and you're not sick. Baker says sometimes they don't even give patients individual treatment, they just put them on these standard protocols to see what happens.'

'I don't think that's true. It's one of the best cancer hospitals in the world. Of course they have to do some research – after all they're trying to cure cancer as well as treat it. But they care about patients a lot. You'll see when you meet Mack Riley.'

'I hope I never see him.'

'You'd like him, really.'

'He's a chemotherapist; I don't want to go through that. I don't want chemotherapy, I think I'd rather die. Remember with your father what it was like? Remember that?'

'Of course I remember, it was terrible. But it wouldn't be the same, Mom, it isn't the same kind of cancer, you don't have the same disease he did.'

'Cancer is cancer.

'Not really, cancer is dozens of different diseases, just the way there are different kinds of flu, or lots of different kinds of bacterial infections.'

'Dr. Baker said they use the patients as human guinea pigs, they just treat them . . . oh no!' her mother interrupted herself, 'I forgot all about the soup, and now it's boiling over, I'll talk to you later, dear, thanks for calling.' The line went dead.

· 25 ·

'Who is this joker Harold Baker?' Kate asked. It had taken her half an hour to get through to Riley on the telephone.

'Hal Baker? Where did you run into him?'

'I didn't. He's been telling my mother what a terrible place Parkinson is, how you have a surgeon who cuts people in half, how you treat patients like guinea pigs, how all you care about is research. It's not very helpful.'

Riley burst out laughing. 'I hope you defended us,' he said.

'It wasn't so easy.'

'Well, I guess Hal's a little bitter. He got fired a few years ago, he didn't do enough research, didn't write enough papers, failure to sufficiently detach, you know. He's not a bad guy actually.'

'I wish he'd keep his mouth shut.'

'That was another of his problems, talking to patients.'

'That's against the rules?'

'It depends what you say. I don't know, maybe Hal has a point, some days this place is pretty awful.'

'But you don't use patients as guinea pigs.'

'No, but we do sometimes care more about how a patient responds because of what it will mean to research than because of how they feel. I mean, it just happens,' he said.

'I don't think you do that, look at the way you feel about Dorothy Clay.'

Riley was silent for a minute. 'But even with the patients I care about, I'm often helpless,' he said. 'Dorothy's gone down to a clinic in Mexico where they do enzyme injections. The chemotherapy wasn't working.'

'She has? Isn't that illegal?'

'No, alternative treatments are not illegal. Some doctors don't aprove of them, but in this case, we weren't helping her, and Hector Portillo who runs the clinic isn't a quack or anything. I don't know if it helps, but he used to work here.'

'He used to work here, and now he's running one of these laetrile clinics?'

'Not laetrile, Kate, it's a medical clinic, and he thinks he's found a substance that does work,' Riley said. He remembered Hector Portillo, a wealthy South American who had gone through Yale and come to Parkinson. He had been too Latin, too passionate for the bureaucracy. The frustration got to him. Since he had the money, he had set up his own labs, found something that seemed to work and left.

'*Does* it work?' Kate asked. 'They've cured cancer, and you're not telling us?'

'Sometimes it does work,' Riley said. 'But in the cases I've seen, the remissions are temporary. In the end it comes out about the same, but people are very encouraged when they can see tumors get smaller on the X-rays. They don't think about the tumors coming back.'

'I can understand that, but doesn't it make you feel odd, that your patient has gone for this?'

'Maybe, I guess my attitude is, more power to her. Dorothy Clay isn't a woman who gives up, and that's what I like about her. She has something to fight.'

'All of your patients have something to fight; they don't all go to Mexico.'

'It's true, there aren't a lot of healthy people in here. It's been a bad morning, in fact, everyone's worse, everyone's acting a little nuts.' Even Eddie Gomez had been silent that morning. Riley had passed Mrs. Gomez on her way to the elevators, and she had burst into tears. Riley had comforted her, but by the time he got to Eddie's room, he didn't have the energy to bring the little boy around. If he couldn't make Eddie feel better, who would? He was left with the image of Eddie sitting silently in the chair where the nurse had propped him with the treasured baseball cap tilted down over his eyes. He didn't want to talk.

'Does that bother you?' Kate asked.

'Yes and no. I feel badly when I can't help, but I understand. Who knows how any of us would act if we were that sick. I might decompensate pretty badly if someone told me what I have to tell patients.'

'*Decompensate?*'

'You know, fail to compensate, fall apart, what's the matter with that?'

'Nothing, I just don't think it's a word.'

'It certainly is around here,' Riley said.

'Sure, you guys have your own language, a combination of medical terminology and words like *decompensate*. The point is that no one else can understand it – it keeps you insular, keeps your secrets safe.' In the background she could hear Riley's radio. She knew he was leaning back in his desk chair, trying to relax. It was a violin and piano piece, very cool.

'What do you mean we have our own language? It's English, anyone can learn it.'

'But they don't, that's the point. It's English, but most people don't understand half of what you say. When you go to medical school, you learn this foreign language as well as everything else. It keeps other people at a distance. Even the grammar is different. I mean,' Kate imitated a doctor's low, authoritative voice, '"we have an LOL with ascites and a second acute MI," that's not the way most people talk. You use initials a lot too. I read somewhere that when someone is finally dying the doctors say they are CTD.'

'Even I don't know what that means.'

'Circling the drain,' Kate said.

'Do you want to teach me grammar, or do you want to tell me how unfeeling we are?'

'I'm sure you know grammar, I'm sure you know the rules,' Kate said, 'what's a compound sentence?'

'I like your spirit.'

'Wrong, that's a simple sentence.'

· III ·

'Okay, how about . . . "I know the rules, but my feelings are important."'

'Good, it can be shorter than that, too.' Kate was sitting in her office at the rickety pine table which had been the kitchen table at home when she was a child. When she had found her office, her father had refinished it for her, and there were still patches of the old finish raised like the map of a mysterious archipelago across one leaf. She remembered him out on the broad back porch in his worn corduroys sanding and staining. It was his silent way of giving her career his blessing – or at least she hoped so. '"Stop and think," is a compound sentence,' she said.

'Does it have to have a comma?' he asked. In the background Kate heard another telephone ringing, and the high, pinging noise of a beeper going off. The music stopped. 'Can you hold on a moment?' Riley asked.

While she waited, cradling the receiver against her shoulder, Kate looked around her office in the morning light. Geraniums and ivy bloomed on the roofs of the Upper East Side. Across the street from her building, someone was knocking out the walls of a penthouse to add a greenhouse. Three men in overalls dismantled the old brick cornices with hammers and chisels. A sheet hung in front of another hole to keep out the dust. In the distance she could see other penthouses with their weight of unnatural greenery, willow and apple trees bowing over the edges of buildings, and a huge white pine at the corner of a granite building over on Madison plunging upward toward the sky.

'Sorry,' Riley was back on the telephone. 'What were we saying?'

'You wanted to know, let's see, you wanted to know if a compound sentence has to have a comma, and the answer is no, but it can.'

In the background, the music started again, some kind of violin concerto came wafting through the receiver.

'He said he was in love with her comma,' Riley said, 'and she was a married woman.'

'You *know* the rules,' Kate said.

'That doesn't mean I have to like them.'

'It can have a different conjunction too, like but,' she said. '"She wanted him passionately, but he was afraid."'

'Or, "She was a very attractive woman, but the situation made things impossible,"' he said. 'What's a complex sentence, then?'

'A sentence with a subordinate clause,' she said. 'Like, "I won't be happy until I see you again."'

'Or, "I didn't think I could feel this way before I met you."' he said.

'That's right,' she said, 'and a compound-complex sentence is, "I didn't think I could feel this way before I met you, but . . ."'

'"But I'm afraid we could get into a lot of trouble,"' he said.

'"What are we doing?" That's a simple sentence,' she said.

'The sentence is simple,' he said, 'the answer . . .'

'Is not so simple.'

'We think the same way,' he said.

'Now you know everything about grammar, you're an enlightened man, the only English-speaking doctor at the hospital, doesn't that feel good?'

'I certainly feel better than I did when you called,' Riley said. 'You've really cheered me up. Let's have lunch, okay? How about Tuesday?'

'Yes,' Kate said, 'that's simple.' He laughed. The music had stopped now, and she could hear the beeper going off and the telephones ringing.

'I have clinic in the morning, come meet me here about twelve-thirty, just go to the patients' waiting room where you found me before.'

'Meet you in clinic?'

'You know, where you waited with your father, I'll be there.'

'Okay,' she said.

Kate hung up, leaned back in her chair and looked out at the blue summer sky above the roof tops. 'I didn't know I could feel this way,' he had said. On the couch in his apartment, he had been carried away by her physically, overcome by his desire, even if he *had* gotten control of himself at the last minute. Perhaps it was better to build up anticipation so that when they finally did sleep together, the pleasure would be more intense. It would probably happen in her apartment, the first time at least. Over there on the daybed. They would be sitting and talking, and he would stand up and walk over to her and take her hand.

They wouldn't have to say a word.

· 26 ·

Kate walked down Lexington Avenue through humid midsummer air which seemed to smear heat and dampness against her skin. She wore a blue linen shift, and her dark hair was pulled back into a thick braid, but by the time she got to 79th Street, she felt rumpled and hot and beads of sweat poured down her back. She stepped to the edge of the sidewalk to avoid the beggar who sold pencils in front of the deli and caught her heel for a moment in the subway grating. A huge waterbug scuttled under the coping of the coffee shop opposite the subway station, and a rivulet of dirty water from dripping air conditioners wound across the pavement to the street. She tucked her gold chain inside the neck of the dress, the newspaper had had a story yesterday about women having their jewelry snatched off their necks by robbers who whizzed by on bicycles. As she turned onto 78th Street and past the row of brownstones to Park, Kate walked under the trees on the north side. In the shade, she pushed her sunglasses back on her head. This was the street where she had gone so often to Ricardo Charles's little, one-room apartment in the big, brick building on the corner. She wondered if the doorman recognized her, or if she would see Ricardo walking his latest lady hurriedly in under the canopy. Of course Ricardo never risked that. He had always met here there and then had her leave before he did. It seemed like a long time ago.

As she walked into the hotel restaurant on Madison, a blast of cold air just inside the glass doors cooled her skin and cleared her head. Ann Lacey was sitting on a curved velvet banquette under a huge arrangement of irises and lilies. The businesslike richness of her gray suit was lightened by two long strands of pearls.

'Hi!' Ann smiled and stood to kiss her. 'Sorry to drag you to such a dreary place,' she said. 'it's just so convenient.'

'And so cool,' Kate said. She sank into the luxurious softness of the banquette and ordered some expensive water.

'I asked Mack to drop by if he had time,' Ann said, 'fat chance.'

'He once told me he took that job so he'd be busy all the time, so he wouldn't have to think too much,' Kate said. Talking with Ann about Mack was dangerous, dangerous but interesting. Kate wanted to know everything about Macklin Riley, and especially everything about his connections with other women. She wanted to know if he had ever flirted with Ann, if he had ever talked to her about himself the way he had talked to Kate, if he had ever kissed her. Of course she couldn't ask, and Ann wouldn't tell. Kate felt a great affection for Ann Lacey because of all they had in common, and it was both heightened and inhibited by her sense that they were both pursuing the same man.

'Tell me about it,' Ann laughed. 'He's not exactly introspective. Still, I think he's becoming more thoughtful, or maybe that's just what I hope.'

'I think you're right, I think we're meeting him at a time when he's changing,' Kate said. The possibility that Riley might appear at any moment, however remote, made her preen every time she heard footsteps approaching the dining room. She hoped he wouldn't come; she didn't want him to see how great Ann Lacey looked. She hoped he would come; she wanted to see him.

'But how much, how much can someone like that change? I think he wants to change, he certainly wants to be more successful; he wants more power, but is that change? Let's order,' Ann nodded to the headwaiter.

'God, I don't know. He's barely separated, that ought to make a difference.'

Ann ordered a salad and Kate did too. 'Do you think he fucks around?' Ann said. Kate wondered if the headwaiter was out of earshot, but Ann didn't seem to care.

'Interesting question,' she said, 'but they're not supposed to fool around with patients or with patients' families, are they?' She remembered Mack going cold as she straddled him on the sofa in his apartment. 'It's not a good idea,' he had said, 'not for a lot of reasons.' Now she wondered if one of the reasons was Ann Lacey.

'They're not supposed to, but a lot of them do, there have been plenty of cases at Parkinson of doctors marrying patients, that kind of stress can be sexy. There are all these young nurses, young women doctors, I think it's pretty tempting.'

'Don't you think Riley's too uptight for that? Don't you think he would consider it unethical?'

Ann shrugged. 'He might, for a while. There are usually ways to convince yourself that something is ethical if you want to do it enough.' Kate looked across the room toward the door, a group of businessmen were going over sheaves of paper at one table while their lunches cooled. At another, a family, two blonde parents and two little girls dressed in frills and bows, attacked huge desserts.

'But would he want to?'

Ann didn't answer but picked at her salad. 'I don't know,' she said finally. 'I don't think he's rigid about hospital rules and regulations, but I don't know about sex. There's only one way to find out.' She looked up and grinned. Kate tried to smile back.

'Well, you or me?' she said, trying to sound as joking and unconcerned as Ann did.

'We'll have to flip a coin,' Ann said, 'do you want some coffee?'

'Sure, don't you think it's odd the way we both met him? Do you think he knows lots of other women whose mothers he's treating?'

Ann shrugged. 'I don't know,' she said, 'there's no one like my mother.'

'It must be nice to feel that way,' Kate said. Once again she felt envious of Ann Lacey, of her closeness to her mother.

'How's it going with your mother?' Ann asked.

'She's nervous, she's about to start radiation. She keeps herself incredibly busy; that's her way of denying that there's anything wrong with her.'

'Radiation, God, I remember that with nostalgia now, it's amazing what we can adjust to. When people who've known my mother for a long time see her now, they're shocked. I mean, she's lost her hair and everything. She looks wonderful to me though, I'd be happy if she could just stay this way.'

'How was Mexico? Did you go down with her?'

'No, I wanted to, but my aunt, my father's sister, went instead. It encouraged her a lot. At first the drugs – they're called enzyme activators – seemed to work, they seemed to be shrinking the tumors.'

'Great, can you get more of it?'

'That's not the problem, it's not working as well now. I don't know.'

'One day at a time,' Kate said. She saw a reflection of herself in Ann, the traces of an ordeal that she might be facing with her own mother. For a moment, she felt Ann's frustration and helplessness.

'That's easier some days than others,' Ann said, her voice had dropped. 'But thanks.'

'Are you staying in this afternoon?' Kate asked. Ann signed the check with a scrawl of signature before Kate could protest. She scrounged in her wallet for the cash to pay half, but Ann waved dismissively. 'Do you want to go shopping?'

'No damn, I have another meeting.' Ann glanced at her thin gold watch; she was wearing cuff links in the shape of tiny blue and gold knots. 'I guess our friend isn't going to show,' she said.

'Busy, busy,' Kate said.

He's helped us a lot, I'm concentrating on remembering that,' Ann said.

'I'm sure you've helped him too.'

'I don't see how, except that just knowing us is such a privilege, and except for the paintings.

'The paintings?'

'Oh God, didn't I tell you. Remember those paintings, that artist named Mina Jonque? He told my mother about her and showed her some slides, and she insisted that we buy four of them. "We have offices to decorate," she said. That woman is so perverse!' Kate wished she had that kind of affection for her own mother's perversity.

'You bought those paintings?' Kate asked.

'People do what they have to do,' she said and then laughed. 'Listen, I have to go, I've got to visit Mummy, and there's another meeting in the morning. I have to stay in town again tonight. We're acquiring a television station, for God's sake, can you believe it? It was Daddy's idea, but he's not here of course. It's a lot of work for the lawyers, and me too.'

As Kate walked uptown to her apartment, she wondered if Ann had a dinner date with Macklin Riley. She would be in town; he would be in town. She imagined them sitting thigh to thigh on a banquette somewhere in a restaurant that Ann knew about. Candlelight, red wine. In the meantime, Kate would be sulking in her squalid room with Madam Barthélemy shrieking outside the door. Or she would be sitting at the dining-room table in silence, eating with a man she no longer loved. Their forks would clink against their plates as they ate the chicken salad that she had bought because she didn't care enough to cook. Afterward David would have a scotch and fall asleep on the sofa. Kate crossed Park Avenue. Two boys on skateboards were racing each other down the slope from 86th Street, slaloming in and out between the cars.

Ann Lacey could sit at the head of a conference table and tell lawyers what to do. Ann Lacey could buy and sell most people. She could donate a building to the hospital or give the money for a laboratory. She and her mother had bought some of Mina Jonque's paintings! She was someone who knew just how to get what she wanted. And if she wanted Macklin Riley. . . ? Even if she didn't really want him, she would probably acquire him just to stay in practice. After their dinner together, Kate imagined them going up in the elevator to Ann's hotel suite. They'd have a drink and joke about the complimentary chocolates on the pillow, and in the end they'd roll together in the soft sheets turned down by the night maid. Kate felt a sudden, sharp sense of loss, a familiar imbalance which tipped her toward depression. As she turned onto Lexington Avenue, cars honked and a bicyclist sped up the street in the wrong direction.

· 27 ·

Ann Lacey bent over her mother's bed, pushing the IV tubing aside and pressing against the high hospital rails. She had knocked on the half-opened door and called 'hello' in a cheery voice, but her mother was asleep, breathing noisily through her slack open mouth. Although Mack kept assuring her that her mother had a chance, she couldn't imagine anyone looking closer to death. Her skeleton, those 'great bones', seemed to be just beneath the skin of her forehead and her scalp, where tufts of hair were growing back from her last chemotherapy treatment. Her hand on the sheet was as light as a small bird, and she didn't wake or stir when Ann picked it up. The wrist felt stiff and fragile, as if it might break off under the tender pressure of her daughter's grasp.

Dorothy Clay's eyes were blue. Ann often thought it was the same blue as the sea around Frenchman's Bay at the end of Logan Point on the island at home. Lately the color had seemed to be leaking out of her mother's eyes, and more and more she seemed to be looking inside herself, or looking at nothing at all. Her breathing was uneven, as if each breath had a long, hard journey to go from her lungs to the air outside, and there were fits and starts as it encountered obstacles and overcame them – for the moment.

Ann sat down on the turquoise chair next to the bed and reached through the bars to put a hand on her mother's head. It was so small. She tried to will her own youth and strength into her mother's body. She had never prayed much, but now she found herself pleading inwardly with someone or something. Out the window she could see the East River and the low buildings across it. Her mother had gone to church every Sunday. Sometimes Ann had gone with her, just for company, and now she strained to remember the prayers she had heard many times and forgotten. 'Come unto Me all ye that travail and are heavy laden,' she remembered, 'and I will refresh you.' It didn't seem quite right. She prayed for the 'Peace of God which Passeth All Understanding.' Down the river she could see the boxy, gray buildings on Roosevelt Island. She and Scott had taken the tram over there once for a walk. It depressed her. All that uniformity. All those neat, identical places to live. It had been a spring day though, and the island itself seemed like a ship. She had been so happy to be with Scott, handsome Scott. Now she wondered where he was, and if he was doing something at the office that she would have to undo.

Those days with Scott had been so charged with passion. Now he was a liability. He had had so much to teach her about her own body, but now she had to excite herself with fantasies when he wanted to sleep with her. He had other outlets, she knew, little secretaries, some of the buying assistants in Florida and California. Women he had hired, who now obliged him.

She noticed that one of the flower arrangements on the table by the windowsill was dying. It was a traditional one, roses and irises in a cut-glass vase, which she had put next to the pot of daisies the Weavers had sent. She picked up the heavy vase, dumped the flowers in the big wastebasket she had bought for the bathroom, and rinsed it out, turning the vase in the tiny sink to free it of the green rings on the glass. 'Flowers,' she wrote in her rounded hand at the top page of her agenda; she would get some more this afternoon after Riley came. In the hall outside, she heard the noise of a doctor doing rounds, the shuffle of feet and the chatter of voices, as the doctor, followed by his entourage of obsequious students and residents, traveled from room to room. Shuffle, shuffle, chatter, chatter, then a low drone as the doctor made his pronouncements and everyone listened as if they were prophecy. Thank God for Mack who came, when he came, alone.

Carefully, because her mother must not know how much

arranging went into keeping this bleak room bright, Ann weeded the old magazines out of the antique wooden rack she had brought from home and replaced them with new ones. On the table she put a fresh box of chocolate truffles. Mack and her mother shared a taste for sweet things.

The hospital was like a prison. There was no privacy. Everything was institutionalized, even the sheets and pillow cases were stamped with the hospital seal. Next door, a woman started to scream. Ann went out into the hall; a knot of doctors and nurses crowded the entrance to the room next door.

'How long is that likely to go on?' Ann asked one of the nurses. The noise might wake her mother, wake her to a woman screaming.

'Oh, there's nothing you can do about it,' one of the nurses said and turned back into the room. Yes, Ann thought, there is something I can do about it. But she felt paralyzed. Even if she charged into the room and throttled the woman, it wouldn't really make any difference. Her mother wouldn't feel better.

In the hospital, the world closes down into a narrow, vivid focus. Only the hospital seems real. They bring the morning paper, but no one reads it. Life is stripped down to its essentials, like travel in a mountainous, dangerous country. The real world is a small, dark room where people come in and out to prod and poke and ask the same questions over and over, beige walls, beds on wheels, fluorescent lights, meals on trays, chipped paint, the smell of antiseptic, and in the distance the sound of someone screaming.

· 28 ·

'Oh, hi, dear,' Ann's mother's voice was weak and grating. Ann sat back in the chair and reached out to touch her arm, the skin was papery and close to the bone.

'How are you feeling?'

'You look wonderful, sweetie. Have they decided anything? Is Mack coming with the enzyme stuff?'

'He's supposed to be here soon, but he gets busy, you know.'

'You should call him, have lunch with him sometimes, Annie, don't you think he's attractive?' Her mother's mind skipped from subject to subject these days. Her voice was stronger as she spoke, teasing her daughter seemed to have brought her back to life.

'Hey, I'm married!' Ann laughed, although they both knew that this was less and less true.

'Well, a little flirtation . . . never mind, it's just an old woman's fantasy, you can't blame me for dreaming,' her mother said. Ann had always loved her mother's ability to talk as if she were a much younger woman, to talk as if she were a friend as well as a mother. When she had become engaged to Scott, her mother had advised her, gently, against marrying someone from a different background, no matter how wonderful he might be. Ann had been determined, she usually was, and Dorothy had given in with grace and become as supportive and affectionate toward her son-in-law as anyone could be. So affectionate, in fact, that Scott really thought Dorothy was on his side and had tried recently to invoke her support in arguments against Ann. A tactical error. Now that her mother had turned out to be right, Ann also appreciated her never saying or even hinting at an 'I told you so.' Instead she felt, as she had always felt, that her mother was her best friend, no matter what she did.

It exhilarated her and made her nervous to talk about Mack Riley with her mother. She was afraid Dorothy might come up with some truth that would shatter her own precious infatuation with the young doctor, some comment that was so perfectly precise and well put that Ann wouldn't be able to avoid it, even in her fantasies. She wasn't sure how she felt about Macklin Riley, or what she wanted from him. She saw his weaknesses, she knew he was in trouble at the hospital. It was clear, to her at least, that his involvement with patients was crippling him as a doctor. At the same time, his presence, his love for her mother, and the possibilities he somehow seemed to represent were saving her from slipping toward despair. Her marriage was over, her father was gone, her mother was dying, and Riley was someone she could lean on as her world collapsed. When she mentioned him, her mother's head came up from the pillow, and a blush of interest suffused her waxy skin.

'I think he's crazy about you, Annie,' she said.

'You're kidding, it's you he has the crush on, he's always going on about how magnificent you are; it's gotten quite boring, and he's in here all the time, even the nurses notice it.'

'Don't be silly, look at me!' Her mother waved a frail hand toward her own head. Of all the losses Ann had seen her mother gallantly bear, even the loss of her husband to Europe, business, and incidental women, Ann had seen that the loss of her hair was the hardest. They had experimented with wigs. Ann had bought a series of bandboxes with samples from various wig makers to the hospital, but Dorothy always complained that they were uncomfortable, or that they didn't look right. She had treated her wonderful hair so casually when she had it, pulling it into a glossy roll at the back of her neck. The truth was, no wig could match its richness or its luster.

'Mummy, he loves you for yourself,' Ann said.

'Well, that would be a change.' Ann had never heard her mother complain about her father – even indirectly. Her parents always seemed to get along perfectly, especially when they were apart. For the past fifteen years, maybe longer, Ann's father, Adam Choate Clay, had spent most of his time in Rome, where he had a small palazzo on the Via del Plebiscito near the Piazza Venezia, and in London, where he had a flat in Belgravia.

When Dorothy Clay had been diagnosed as having breast cancer, before the first operation her father had come home on the Concorde, making a big fuss over speed when in fact it was too late. At first he was very solicitous; the hospital room was filled with flowers, there was an extra private nurse, and a lot of visitors who seemed to alternately bore and tire her mother. After about a month, when it was clear that the first operation was not going to be the end of the problem, and the adjuvant chemotherapy had been scheduled, he went back to Europe. Ann remembered one of the doctors describing how husbands behave when their wives get cancer. 'Zoooom,' he had said.

Her father had always been a distant and glamorous figure, a name on the Fortune 500 list and in the society columns. Even when Ann was growing up, at home on Turk Cay, her father was always off on some business trip or important expedition. He was stalking in Kenya or shooting in Scotland, or attending a high-level economics meeting in Bonn. When he did come home, it was with a planeload of friends, men named Reggie and Teddy who headed straight for the tennis court and the pool and the bar, and elongated girls named Mandy and Susie who hung on them like gorgeous trailing vines.

'Anyway,' Ann said, 'isn't Dr. Riley still legally married?'

'He is? I think he said they had signed the separation papers.'

'Great! Is that what you two talk about when I'm not around? He's supposed to be discussing your blood gases and your white-cell count for God's sake.'

'Sometimes we talk about you,' her mother grinned.

'And what do you say?'

'You'll have to ask him; I think he'd enjoy telling you. You know his wife was the girl next door, his childhood sweetheart, everyone's entitled to one mistake.' Now her mother's voice trailed off. Ann was about to say that she hadn't allowed herself the one mistake that she gave others. She had stayed with Adam Clay and made the best of it, so well that no one knew she was making the best of it. But her mother was staring up at the van Gogh reproduction on the wall and Ann could tell her thoughts had gone inward again. A reaper in the sunset. The print had faded so that the rich gold and brilliant blue of the original painting were a barely distinguishable yellowy beige.

'I don't like being here, Annie, I think I'm worse.' Her mother was lying back again, speaking up toward the ceiling in a harsh whisper. There was a soft knock on the door and Macklin Riley walked into the room. Ann's heart jumped. He was always there, just when she needed him.

'You girls gossiping? I don't want to interrupt anything,' he said. Dorothy's face took on some color and she smiled again.

'No, no,' she said, 'we're glad to see you.' Riley sat on the edge of the bed and took Dorothy Clay's wrist in his hand. His touch seemed to infuse her with life and energy. She shifted on the pillows and sat up. Ann saw that he was carrying one of the bottles from Tehualtepec Clinic and a package of syringes.

'Always ready to talk, aren't you, Dorothy?' he said. 'Don't you miss me and the nurses when I send you home?'

Dorothy Clay laughed. 'I do, I do miss you,' she said, 'but it's worth it. If you were there, that would be perfect.'

'Unfortunately,' Riley said, 'they insist on giving me other patients. Poor me.'

'And lucky them,' Dorothy Clay said. 'Do I see a bottle in your hand? Do you think that stuff really works?'

'It did seem to work,' Riley said, standing up and walking around the bed to the IV pole. 'It's up to you, Dorothy.'

'I have to take it,' she said, 'even if it's just in case.'

Riley tore open the package of syringes and plunged one of them into the rubber cap of the bottle, pulling out half a syringeful. He unlinked the IV tube and relinked it to the glucose mixture. Ann watched his hands which seemed to have a confidence and surety of their own. He inserted the syringe in the measured cylinder next to the bag on the IV pole and pushed the plunger, the red enzyme activator spurted into the white mixture in clouds, tinting it pink.

'I can't figure out if you approve of this or not,' Ann said to Riley's back.

'I want your mother to be happy,' he said.

'I guess we shouldn't tell anyone you're doing this.'

Riley shrugged and relinked the tubing to the glucose and medicine bags.

'You could get into a lot of trouble, couldn't you?' Ann said.

'I'll be back to see her in a couple of hours,' Riley said, turning to Ann now. His gaze was absolutely neutral. She smiled, but instead of smiling back he reached out and touched her arm. 'Take care,' he said, and before she had a chance to respond, he was gone.

'He certainly cheers me up,' her mother said from the bed, 'and at least there aren't any of those terrible side effects with this stuff.' Ann could see that Riley's departure had already robbed her of the burst of energy she had had when he came into the room. 'It's odd, seeing Riley, because I like him so much, it makes me homesick.'

'Mummy, no one likes being in the hospital. It's a depressing place.' Ann tried to lift her mother's mood, but she was aware that her best efforts had a fraction of the effect of Dr. Riley's presence.

'What if I don't get better?'

'Mummy, don't think that way, of course you're going to get better, you're getting better.'

'I wonder, I wonder if he would tell me the truth. . . . I don't want to put anyone through too much, it might take a long time.'

'I'm glad to be able to take care of you for once, all the times you took care of me.'

'There's some Dilaudid in the medicine cabinet at home. I'd like it to be at home, not here where no one knows me.'

The door to the room was pushed open with a bang, and a dark-haired nurse bustled in.

'And how are we this afternoon, Mrs. Clay?' she chirped. 'I see we have a visitor!' She pulled a thermometer out of its bright blue casing and popped it into Dorothy Clay's mouth. The conversation was over.

· 29 ·

'Tell the one about the duck!' Andrea Lucci was practically jumping out of her skimpy nurse's uniform with excitement. Dr. Peter Mallory nodded as he made notes from the pile of charts at the tenth-floor station. Andrea reminded him of the cheerleaders at high school. All the pretty girls had been Italian – and scrawny Peter Mallory had been Irish.

'Just for you, Andrea,' he said. His resident and the new medical student stopped reading to listen; it certainly wasn't hard to get them to take a break. Another nurse came over from the computer at the corner of the room.

'Four doctors go on a hunting trip, an internist, a psychiatrist, a surgeon and a pathologist,' Mallory said. He remembered Dr. Latham telling this joke up at Harvard. Old Latham, before he won the Nobel, before he had the heart attack, before he had sent his brightest protétége out into the world of surgery and politics.

'A bird flies over. It's the internist's turn to shoot. "Ahh," he thinks, "it looks like a duck, webbed feet, pin feathers . . ." But by the time he determines that it is a duck, the bird is gone.

'Another bird flies over and it's the psychiatrist's turn to shoot. "Hmmmm," the psychiatrist thinks, "it looks like a duck, but does it *feel* like a duck?" and while he thinks, the bird flies off.

'A third bird is flushed. The surgeon raises his oiled equipment and gets off a perfect shot before the duck is more than a few feet off the ground. The surgeon turns to the pathologist. "Jack," he says, "go and see if that's a duck."'

Ignoring the laughter as he finished the joke, Mallory swung back into gear. He usually did two or three things at once. Standing in the nurses' station, he flipped through notes on patients and took a telephone call from a colleague who asked him to look in on a patient. A nurse handed him a piece of cherry cheesecake on a paper plate, and he spooned it into his mouth with a plastic fork as he talked. Breakfast. Still eating the cheesecake, he charged out into the hall followed by his resident, and on the way into the first patient's room, he threw the remains of the cake in the trash.

Mrs. Waters, the first patient on rounds, was a woman who had had a peritoneal resection a week ago. She was well enough to go home. Most patients' rooms were festooned with cards, photographs, flowers, and the other gift shop tokens representing good wishes. Mrs. Waters was alone with the plant that the Gray Ladies had brought on the day of her operation. Its leaves were curling and brown. There was nowhere to send her, she was still too sick to live alone in her apartment, but Mallory needed the bed for sicker patients.

'Doesn't she have any family?' the new resident asked.

'Oh sure, but they don't want her,' Mallory said.

'You're kidding.' The new resident was blond with a round, baby face. 'Why don't you just release her?'

'You heard me, they wouldn't come. They'd leave her sitting in the lobby, you've got to learn to listen,' Mallory tried not to let his impatience show. Eventually the hospital's social services would find a place for Mrs. Waters, probably a state nursing home, but that might take a week.

'I think that's terrible,' the resident said, personally outraged. Mallory let it go. Either this guy would learn what people were like, or he wouldn't. He'd be rotated off Mallory's service in a month anyway, on to work for some other lucky doctor.

The second patient was Mr. Krupo, a wizened man who wore a knitted cap to hide his baldness. Mallory knew that Krupo was a real estate man from Brooklyn, a friend of Frank Sinatra, a resident of Palm Springs in the winter, but the disease had stripped him of decades of assimilation, and he had the sharp, wrinkled face of a peasant.

Last week, Mallory had performed an emergency operation on him and extended his probable life span from a few days to a few months. After that Mr. Krupo had been the happiest man in the hospital – as if his brief reprieve from death was more precious than a lifetime. But today his thoughts seemed to have caught up with him. He complained angrily that he hadn't had a bowel movement.

Mallory sat down in the visitor's chair. He had to be in the Operating Room in ten minutes. Dan Connors was already being put under and the residents scrubbed for the operation Mallory would perform.

'No bowel movement?' Mallory said. 'Now who can tell me what is the average frequency of the American bowel movement?' The nurse and the resident didn't know. Mr. Krupo didn't know.

'The United States Marines did a randomized study and found that the average American bowel movement occurs from three times a day to three times a week. So you see, my friend,' he said to Krupo, 'you're average.'

The information didn't seem to cheer up Joe Krupo. 'I have these cramps and churnings in my stomach,' he said.

'Oh, come on,' Mallory cajoled him, 'I have those too!'

Krupo looked grim. 'I wish I had your churnings,' he said.

Mallory got up off his chair. He knew when to give in.

'You're right, my friend,' he said, all seriousness and sympathy, 'you're right.' He laid a hand on Krupo's bony shoulder. The old man shivered in his flannel nightshirt although the room was hot. He would be dead before the end of the summer; Mallory pushed the thought away.

In the OR, Dan was draped and ready. Carefully Mallory opened the flesh above the abdominal cavity. Cut and clamp, cut and clamp, until the organs were visible. In the OR, Mallory's senses always seemed to sharpen no matter how tired he was. Over the hiss of the suction, he could hear the sounds of feet passing in the hall outside, the nurse's breathing as she stood next to him.

Mallory probed the intestines with his hands. The disease had grown over the bowel, it was not the isolated red fleshy tumor he had hoped for. Still, he would be able to bypass the obstruction by anastomosing the loops of bowel, cutting them and restitching them together, and, at least for a while, Dan would be able to eat and nourish what was left of his body. The diseased loop of the bowel cut neatly from the rest, Mallory pushed the intestines aside and looked in toward the spleen. A spattering of white spots covered the upper organs, as if they had been casually splattered with dirty snow. There was nothing he could do about that.

'Let's sew our way out of here,' he said to the nurse. She laughed, and the sound made him feel better. He started to suture the layers of flesh and begin the journey from the body's interior to the outer layers.

· 30 ·

After the operation, Mallory stuffed his surgical greens into the hamper, changed from his clogs back into brown lace-up shoes, put on a fresh white coat, and hurried down to the room where he conducted his teaching conference once a week. It was a big room at street level, with gray, metal, folding chairs and gold-flecked, fireproof curtains shutting out the light. There was a platform with a podium at the front of the room, but Mallory avoided it. Instead, he moved around so that it was impossible to tell where his questions would come from. 'And what do you think this is?' he asked one student, interrupting a discussion of an abdominal resection in a seventy-two-year-old man. He pointed to a line across a slide projected at the front of the room. 'What do you think that is, Dr. Roberts?' Everyone past the second year of medical school insisted on being called 'doctor'. Mallory fulfilled this protocol so exactly that he was clearly making fun of it.

'That's the hepatic vein, sir,' Roberts answered. He was a tall, slender man, with red hair.

'You think *that* is the hepatic vein? Does anyone else in this room think that is the hepatic vein?' Standing in the aisle at the center of the room, Mallory registered disbelief. Only a perfect fool, an absolute simpleton, someone beyond all hope, would identify this line as the hepatic vein, his voice implied. Roberts faltered and studied the slide again.

'Yes, sir,' he said finally, 'that is the hepatic vein.'

'Right,' Mallory agreed, and he was on to the next question.'

There was a big urn of coffee and plates of brownies and

cookies on the table at the back of the room. The doctors munched away, brushing the crumbs off their lab coats as they listened. Macklin Riley stood in the dark at the back. Mallory probably controlled his future at the hospital, so he came to conference, but he didn't feel like answering questions. Eddie Gomez wasn't responding to the treatment. Janie Bradley, a thirty-two-year-old woman with ovarian cancer, was much worse. Somehow the way she had looked as she tossed on the pillow, and the photographs of her children smiling on the table beside her had gotten to him during rounds this morning. One of the kids had brown pigtails and a gap in her teeth, and she wouldn't have a mother. Was that fair? Riley had reached out to rub some dried saliva off Janie's lips with his thumb and she had moaned at the touch – at human contact – and for a moment he had imagined making love to her.

In front of him, in the middle of the conference room, he could see David Withington sitting quietly in his chair on the aisle. Mallory had taken over Withington's job, and although Mallory was great – he really was – sometimes Riley missed the slow, deliberately gentlemanly pace of the old department. Withington breathed in and out with a low rasp, and Riley saw that he was asleep.

There was an obbligato of beeping sounds as the doctors were paged, the numbers appeared on the screen at the top of their beepers, and the doctors headed for the phone. The trick was to act as if every call was a big emergency, when in fact half the time it was a secretary calling to say that a tuna fish sandwich had arrived. Half of medicine was the proper attitude.

Wherever Mallory was, was the center of the room, as he sipped coffee, fired his questions, or materialized behind the podium to read notes over the speaker's shoulder. He was picking on Roberts today, and Roberts was enjoying it – showing off his intelligence under fire. Their energy made Macklin Riley feel tired. There were so many people sick upstairs, and when they were gone, there were so many more to come. Dorothy Clay's X-rays showed that the tumor was back. He had agreed to inject her with the drugs from Tehualtepec Clinic, breaking the rules of the hospital, because the drugs had seemed to work. Now they had stopped working, and he was left with his anxiety about the broken rules. Besides that, there was the stack of papers he hadn't written, columns of uncollated information, and the faces of people he hadn't helped, the faces of all those people that no one could help.

It was harder and harder for Riley to muster up the necessary optimism for his patients, the optimism that would help them accept the treatment, the optimism that might even help them stave off the disease. Suddenly Riley was tired of the whole thing – the sickness, the bureaucratic rules and regulations, Mallory's antics, spending summer afternoons in a dark auditorium watching an old man sleep. Maybe he should quit and do something else. Riley laughed at himself. There was nothing else he knew how to do.

· 31 ·

Kate walked across the grass and stepped over the flower bed into the woods. Under the big pines it was suddenly cool, dappled light from high above her fell on the thick carpet of needles strewn with pine cones. In the distance she could hear the sound of a lawn mower. Breathing in the sweet piny smell, she went through the trees to where the ground rose and a smooth, hollowed-out boulder sat at the base of a maverick oak. She sat in the indentation on one side, resting her bare legs on a cushion of moss. This was her private place, and she had never told anyone about it. Not even David, not even her father when he was alive.

From the stone, she could just see the corner of the slate roof, the corner over her own room where she had grown up. Her mother was down the hall getting ready for her first radiation appointment. Kate had come to get her, but the house was in disarray, dishes in the sink, cats meowing because they hadn't been fed, piles of laundry heaped on the washing machine. Her mother wasn't ready, she raced up and down the stairs in a frantic search for this and that. First she had forgotten her glasses, then she couldn't find her purse, then she had lost her cigarettes. Kate's offers of help had been waved away; she wouldn't know where this was, she wouldn't know where that was.

To give her mother time, Kate had gone up into the woods to lie against her rock and daydream up at the lacy pine branches and the patches of sky. Who would take care of any of them? Perhaps Macklin Riley would take care of her. He wanted to. She wanted him to. First they would have a passionate affair and then, and then, what a wonderful life she could have with a man like Macklin Riley. He would protect her and she would teach him. He would know just what to do if she were sick or upset, he would be calm and competent in any emergency. When he traveled, she would go with him; she could do a story while he went to his medical conferences, and then they could play together. Maybe they would go to Paris. He'd like Rousseau, they both had the same kind of primitive, natural force. He'd be impressed by her French, and they'd hurry back to their hotel on the Left Bank, to their little room with a wrought-iron balcony above a garden courtyard, because they couldn't wait to be in each other's arms again. Riley was the one, the man who would understand her as she had always known someone would understand her some day. He could give her the love she needed. A squirrel hopped off a branch and scampered over to another tree. The pine needles on the ground began to prick at Kate's legs. But what if Riley didn't love her, didn't even like her? Who would take care of her then? After a while she stood up, brushed the needles off her shorts, and went slowly back to the house. When she got there, her mother was sitting, waiting for her in the car.

'It's nothing to worry about, Mom,' Kate said. 'Not this time. Dr. Riley says it only takes a minute.'

'What does he know?' her mother said; she sat in stiff silence. Kate chuckled out loud to hide her irritation.

'He's been an oncologist for more than ten years,' she said.

'He's never been a patient. Anyway, if it's nothing, why do they have to do it in the hospital?'

'Because that's where they have the radiation machine. It's just like having an X-ray, Dr. Riley says.'

'Dr. Riley this, Dr. Riley that, what makes you think they know so much? What did they ever do for your father?'

'Mom, it's different, you know it's different. We've had this conversation before.'

'It's still cancer, isn't it?' Her mother sighed. 'I hate not getting to have lunch, I'm hungry. Why can't they let you eat something beforehand for God's sake? It's as if they want to make you uncomfortable.'

'It'll be over in half an hour, Mom. We'll get you something to eat, why don't you think about what you'd like?'

Kate turned the car off Route 117 beyond the shops and gas stations on Main Street, and into the long curved driveway of the hospital. She had driven there many times to see her father. On her right was the old hospital building with its brick facade and white columns. She turned the wheel of the car left toward Wemberg Pavilion, a stucco building with small windows that looked as compact and impersonal as a packing crate. Parking across the street from the building, Kate took a ticket from an attendant in a glass booth. He was an old man with white hair and sweat marks growing below the armpits of his gray shirt.

'He looks hot,' she said, but her mother was slumped in the seat silently, the prisoner of private thoughts and fears. Kate got out and opened the door on her mother's side and helped her out of the car onto the hot asphalt. She smelled tar. Matilda seemed suddenly weakened, as if fear had sapped her energy. Kate took her mother's arm and felt her whole weight descend forward on it.

Inside the hospital, they were directed down a long hall and into a small, empty waiting-room. On one side of the room, a round table was piled with old magazines. It looked as if a lot of people had waited there for a lot of time. Across from the magazine table, a rack was filled with information pamphlets. Chemotherapy: What It Is and What It Does. Mastectomy: Some Questions and Answers About Female Breast Cancer. Twenty-Four Answers to Common Questions About Female Cancer. Matilda looked away from the rack. She sat down heavily on a green sofa and picked up a copy of an old magazine. Kate knew that her mother never read magazines. When she saw Kate reading a magazine, she would often snort with a combination of scorn and contempt. Magazines are a waste of time, she would say, or I don't know how you find time to read that trash. The magazine Matilda was reading was so worn that the pages came away in her hands. She stared straight ahead at an advertisement for mayonnaise.

Kate stepped up to the reception desk. 'My mother, Matilda Loomis, is here for her appointment,' she said. Under the nurse's open white coat, she could see blue jeans and a faded yellow T-shirt with a have-a-nice-day smiling face. The nurse had greasy, black hair and a long face.

'If you'll wait just a moment, we have other patients,' she said. The waiting-room was deserted. She stared at the papers on her desk. When Kate stepped back, the nurse picked up a paperback, *Passion at Twilight*, and began to read. Matilda was silent, she acted as if she had nothing to do with the exchange between her daughter and the nurse. Kate wandered over to the display of pamphlets on cancer and picked one off the rack. Radiation: The Whys and Wherefores. Her mother looked up.

'Oh, Kate, don't,' she said, and Kate dropped the yellow booklet back in its slot.

'Matilda Loomis,' the nurse said in a flat voice. The room was still empty except for the three of them, but the nurse looked around at the unoccupied chairs in order to avoid acknowledging their presence.

'Yes,' Kate presented herself at the desk.

'Are you Matilda Loomis?'

'No, I'm her daughter, she's sitting right there.' Her mother still stared ahead into the pages of the magazine.

'Come on, Mom.' Kate helped her mother out of the chair and over to the desk.

'Here,' the nurse shoved a piece of paper across the desk. 'You have to have a blood test before we can do the radiation.' A room number, 10H, was written on the piece of paper.

'You might have told us, we could have saved time,' Kate said. The nurse picked up her paperback without answering.

· 32 ·

Room 10H was crowded, and Kate and Matilda took their places in a row of plastic chairs. There was nothing to read, but Kate's mother stared straight ahead as if she still had a magazine held in front of her. After almost an hour, they were led into a cubicle by a young man in a white coat with a round face and curly black hair.

'Well, Matilda,' he said, reading her name off a chart held in his chubby hand. 'So we've come for our blood test, have we?' Matilda flinched at his jollity. Kate tried to smile.

'Now give us your arm and just relax,' he said. 'This should only take a minute.'

He palpated the skin inside Matilda's elbow and tied a piece of rubber hosing on her upper arm as a tourniquet.

'This shouldn't hurt more than a tiny bit,' the doctor said, in a high, manic voice, as if he was speaking to a deranged child. He swabbed the skin with alcohol and jabbed the needle of the syringe through the flesh. He pulled back the plunger, but nothing appeared in the syringe. He'd missed the vein.

'Damn,' he said, his face flushing. 'Okay, Matilda, now squeeze your fist hard, as hard as you can.' Again he jabbed the syringe through the skin, again the plunger failed to draw blood into the plastic cylinder.

'Oh, damn!' he said again. 'Let's try that other arm, now just relax, try to relax, Matilda.' He made it clear that his failure to draw blood was her fault. Again he jabbed the needle, harder, Matilda jumped slightly. He released the plunger. Nothing. 'Try not to move,' he said. Kate began to feel nauseous. By the time he was able to draw blood and the precious red drops flowed into the syringe, there were bruises all up and down her mother's arms. Matilda had withdrawn to some silent, frightened place.

Back in the radiation room, a new nurse was on duty. Kate pushed the blue slip with the blood test results across the desk. She was furious. The cure was worse than the disease. But she knew that if she blew up, no one would care. It would only make things worse, waste time, and end up with everything taking twice as long. They would write 'troublemaker' on the chart, and from then on everything would be made even more difficult, if that were possible. The new nurse was pretty and friendly, and Kate watched her mother walk docilely through the door with the radiation danger symbol on it. A few minutes later she walked back out, moving mechanically as if she had stopped feeling, or thinking about what was happening to her.

'How was it, Mom?'

'Hmmmm, what?' Matilda roused herself for a moment, as if she had just noticed that she was not alone.

'Oh, it was fine,' she said.

As she pulled out of the hospital parking lot onto the highway, Kate slowed for the traffic. On the highway she stopped for a red light on a little knoll above the supermarket across from the hospital buildings. She remembered one afternoon when she had dodged cars as she walked across to buy her father some ice cream.

It was after one of the chemotherapy treatments, when her father was propped up against his pillows and still that odd, orangey color he turned after an injection. Suddenly he seemed to feel better, and, in a faint voice, he asked for some strawberry ice cream. But by the time Kate had walked over to the supermarket, stood in line at the check out counter, and brought the ice cream back to the room, her father was asleep, and she didn't want to wake him. She put the ice-cream carton in a saucer that she found in the little pantry at the entrance to his room, but there was no refrigerator, so it melted. Puddles of pink liquid overflowed and dripped down onto the counter top. When Kate left that day, her father was still asleep.

Another time, when she had gone to that hospital to visit her father in the late afternoon, she had found his sheets soaked with blood and puddles of blood dripping on the floor. The resident giving him a blood transfusion had slipped and accidentally torn the plastic bag filled with blood. There was blood on the night table and the books and the flowers and the 'Get Well' cards, and blood on her father's arms and on his blue pajamas, and blood dripping down the metal sides of the bed. Kate knew it was nothing important. It was just another hospital mistake. It wasn't even her father's blood.

'It's no big deal, Dad,' she had said, 'they'll be here to clean it up in a minute. They'll get you another transfusion bag.' She kept her voice casual and cheery, but for days she couldn't get the image out of her head. Her father, covered with blood, dripping with blood. Her father, dying.

· 33 ·

Kate walked slowly up Park Avenue and across 79th Street toward the hospital, past the men in black overalls with their hot-dog and ice-cream carts, and the movie theaters. It was a sunny, early September day, a day out of Norman Rockwell, a day for picking berries in the hot sun and swimming in the sea. The high school that Kate passed at the corner of the avenue looked empty, and iron gratings covered the windows. In the playground behind it, teenaged children were huddled together next to the seesaws, exchanging plastic bags for money. The sharp smell of marijuana filled the air around the swings and the sandbox. On the street, people were eating ice-cream cones.

Kate had been looking forward to her lunch with Macklin Riley, but she dawdled in the sun. As she neared the hospital, her stomach knotted, and her leg felt sore. On the corner she ran into Bert Nevis, an old friend of David's from college days. Normally she would have smiled at him and passed on, but today she stopped and asked about his family and his job and his new house in Connecticut.

At the door to the outpatient wing, Kate passed the attendant who used to help Gideon Loomis into a wheelchair. Her father had hated the wheelchair. He would get slowly out of the car and limp across the sidewalk supported on his cane, with Kate holding him up on the other side. He was determined to walk. But by the time he got to the door of the hospital, he had used up all his strength, and he would allow himself to be lifted into the wheelchair. When this happened, Kate was both relieved and sad. With her father in the wheelchair, everything was more efficient. She could push him where he needed to go. There was no holding him up, no inching along with the rests he needed every ten feet – rests which had to be camouflaged with conversation. Still, it broke her heart. Her father had taught her to walk. When she had been tired of walking, he had carried her high on his strong shoulders.

Waiting for the elevator, Kate stood next to another old man in a wheelchair. The bulletin board across from the elevators was covered with notices, a motorcycle for sale, a showing of *Robin Hood* in the upstairs auditorium, a seminar for the families of cancer patients. Below it a trophy case was filled with the symbols of the staff's prowess at interhospital sports. They had beaten Mount Sinai at golf, they had trounced Beth Israel in tennis, they had won the New York Hospital badminton tournament. Looking down at the old man in the wheelchair as they entered the elevator and started up, Kate thought of her father. Then she realized that the man in the wheelchair was not old, but a young man whose head was bald from chemotherapy and whose body trembled from some neurological disorder. She stepped out of the elevator onto the third floor.

Kate hadn't been at the hospital since she met Macklin Riley, or before that, since she had been there with her father. The dim light of the waiting-room was the same, as if this world existed outside the normal cycle of days and nights, winters and summers. The blank face of the nurse behind the reception desk was the same. The hall was still lined with chairs, and the chairs filled with people waiting, people staring at the wall, people flipping nervously through books or magazines they had brought to read but couldn't concentrate on. Near where Kate had first waited for Dr. Riley, some patients waited on the floor. One woman braced her back against the wall, another sat cross-legged adjusting and readjusting a shiny black wig. Kate asked one of the secretaries for Dr. Riley.

'Not here.'

'Do you know where I can find him?'

The secretary waved toward the other side of the floor without looking up. Kate walked back past the lady on the floor, and the lady with the wig, and down the corridor. A low moan and then a sharp cry of pain came from one of the examining rooms, and suddenly the hospital seemed like the renderings of Hell she had seen in Italian paintings. Crowds of people with their bodies twisted in anguish who waited for time to pass and knew it would never, ever pass. Her father had called it a charnel house, and he was right, it was a death house, a place filled in unbearable misery. Kate felt numb and frightened. Looking up she saw Macklin Riley hurrying toward her down the hall. His white coat was open, his stethoscope jammed in one pocket, his ID card askew. As he rushed toward her, smiling now, other patients' heads turned toward him because he was a doctor and they were hoping that he was coming for them. He wasn't, he was coming for her.

'*There* you are!' he said, turning her down the hall with an arm around her shoulders.

'Hi,' Kate said. She felt so relieved and so grateful that she could hardly get the word out. His arm around her shoulders seemed to shield her from the torment she had seen. He took her elbow and led her past the rows of waiting patients, who had given up again and stared at the wall or at each other.

'It's great to see you. What took you so long? You know your way around here, he chattered as he led her past the last of the examining rooms, past the laboratory where blood was being tested, and through a heavy metal door into another long corridor. Here there were carpets, and silence and no one waiting. These were the doctors' private offices. Kate felt the hush, the absence of chatter and names being called, the almost imperceptible sound of the doctors' voices murmuring behind closed doors. Suddenly a stairway door flew open at the end of the corridor and a tall, sandy-haired doctor burst out of it, followed by two younger men.

'Riley!' the tall doctor called. Riley froze as the other man hurried toward him.

'Did you see the JAMA piece on heparin prophylaxis of DVT?' the tall doctor asked, speaking as rapidly as he walked.

'I'm a little behind on the journals,' Riley said. 'Didn't they combine dihydroergotamine?'

'Mesylate, point five milligrams and five thousand IUs of heparin sodium in a double blind clinical trial,' the tall doctor said. He had reached the spot where Kate and Riley stood, but he didn't stop.

'Are you happy with their RFUTs?' Riley asked.

'The ergotamine complements the heparin, the venotonics discourage hemorrhaging.'

'Post-op procedures?' Riley asked, but the other doctor was already disappearing into an office. Kate could hear telephones ringing and secretaries clamoring for his attention. She and Riley stood in his wake, staring after him.

'Who was that masked rider?' Kate asked. Riley laughed, but he seemed nervous.

'Peter Mallory, my brilliant superior,' he said, 'he's the chief honcho around here.'

'Did I ever mention to you that doctors speak a foreign language?' Kate said. 'Were you looking for an example of that?'

Riley laughed again, more relaxed now, and turned to walk on.

'I guess we do speak a pretty technical language,' he said. His pace in contrast to Peter Mallory's seemed like an amble, his voice sounded like a drawl. Riley's bearish, slow-moving body, his unruly salt and pepper hair, his arm on Kate's shoulder – everything about him looked out of sync with the crisp, emotionless efficiency of the rest of the hospital. Kate followed him down the hall.

· 34 ·

Dr. Macklin Riley's office was a windowless rectangle with a desk at one end, a couch against the wall, and a filing cabinet at the back. The walls were covered with board-and-bracket shelving, stacked with medical journals, books, papers, objects, and bound volumes of documents.

'Was I glad to see you!' Kate flopped down on the couch. 'I'd forgotten what this place is like.'

'I guess it is odd if you come from the outside,' Dr. Riley said as he flipped through a stack of pink message slips. 'Uh-oh, this will only take a minute.' He picked up the receiver of one of two telephones on his desk. 'It's about Mrs. Sanchez, eleven ninety-eight,' he said to someone, 'she's developed ascites.'

'Every available inch of shelf space not crammed with books and papers was covered with miniature, glass figurines, small stone geodes, tea sets, glazed porcelain bowls, and a pair of glass owls. On the shelf directly behind the telephone was a group of plastic, windup animals with instruments, a bear with a snare drum, two monkeys with cymbals, and a cat playing a violin. 'I'd feel more comfortable with a reduced dose of the Adriamycin unless those counts go up, I'll be down later,' Dr. Riley was saying. Kate remembered what the Adriamycin part of the chemotherapy had done to her father, the nausea, what a reduced dose would have meant.

'What's all this *stuff*?' she asked as Riley hung up. 'More collecting?'

'Oh, patients want to give you things,' he said vaguely. 'Here's a pound cake Mrs. O'Rourke baked this morning and brought to clinic,' he waved toward a package covered with ribbons. 'And look at this.' With a flourish he opened his filing cabinet and revealed piles of gift-wrapped, unopened boxes. 'Gloves, neckties, cufflinks, wallets,' he said. In another drawer he showed Kate a dozen bottles of scotch and assorted liqueurs. Beside them were stacks of boxes of chocolate, gold foil-wrapped boxes and silver boxes, and tin boxes painted with pastoral scenes, all untouched and collecting dust.

'I don't know what to do with this stuff,' Dr. Riley said.

Kate remembered buying presents for the doctors with her father, and how important it had seemed to get just the right thing. He took pains to find out what they liked and to provide them with the best of it. Of couse he had never thought about all the other patients doing the same thing. She and her father would go to Brooks, and Tiffany and Steuben, and Sherry-Lehmann shopping for the doctors, and now Kate saw that everyone had the same impulse. The presents seemed to be more than just gifts. They were some kind of sacrificial offering, a propitiation to the most frightening of diseases, an attempt to please, to neutralize, to buy it off.

Now both telephones rang. Riley swore softly and picked one up, putting the other on hold. Kate stood up and walked over to the desk where a heavy, brown book lay open. *Cancer: Principles and Practice of Oncology*, she read across the top cover in gold letters.

'Influence of genetic background . . .' she read. 'To explain the causation of cancer, many theories have been propounded, all of which have sought in various ways to account for the phenotypic changes that typify the cancer cell.' She flipped through the book to the section headed 'Carcinoma of the Endometrium.'

'This is the most common malignant tumor in the female genital tract. . . .' she read. 'Carcinoma of the endometrium has been observed more frequently in Jewish women than in other nationalities; it also may be associated with obesity, hypertension, and diabetes.

'Smith and co-workers have related the development of

carcinoma of the endometrium to an abnormal estrogen balance such as is observed in patients with feminizing ovarian tumors, ... or estrogen therapy for prolonged periods of time. Some recent reports strongly suggest that the prolonged administration of exogenous hormones may be correlated with a greater risk of developing carcinoma of the endometrium, although controversy still surrounds this subject.'

The next pages were filled with graphs showing the frequency of metastases and five-year-survival charts. Kate's eye skipped down the page. 'Approximately 20% of the patients with endometrial carcinoma eventually die of the disease,' she read, 'malignant tumors of the uterus ...'

'Interesting?' Macklin Riley's voice interrupted her reading.

'God, yes, it's all here,' she said. 'Look, they even tell you exactly how to treat it and how to do the surgery and everything.'

'There's very little knowledge that isn't in books, Kate.'

'Somehow I thought ... I guess it was stupid, wasn't it?'

'That doctors were different?' he suggested. 'No, we learn things the same way everyone else does. There's nothing to stop you from going out and buying the books and learning it for yourself – in theory. Of course lab work and experience help a little. Let's get out of here.'

Riley walked from behind the desk and stood just opposite Kate to take off his white coat and put on the blue blazer that was hanging behind the door of his office. As he shrugged out of the white coat, Kate wondered if he imagined that he was taking off his clothes so they could make love. Men thought about sex all the time. She stepped closer, bringing her body against his and putting her arms around him. She stood on tiptoe, tilted her head up, and kissed him on the lips.

'Kate,' he said. His lips were dry, his mouth tasted slightly of peppermint.

'Just a kiss,' she said. Quickly, almost as if he was angry, he squeezed her against him and pushed his tongue between her lips. 'Listen,' he said, drawing back, 'we could get into a lot of trouble.'

'Are you sure it's trouble?'

'I'm sure,' but he kissed her again, and her body felt warm and protected in his arms. He pressed his lips against her closed eyes and mouth. A cart rumbled by in the hall.

'I can tell you one thing,' he said, letting his arms fall slack and stepping backward, 'if and when we ever do sleep together, it will not be in my office here at the hospital.'

'Where will be it?'

'You're asking me more than I know,' he said.

'Do you ever think about it?' Kate stepped toward him again.

'I think about it every time I see you,' he said.

'Well, then?'

'Kate, it would be unethical and unwise. We even say it in the Hippocratic Oath, that we will comfort patients and not abuse them.'

'Who's abusing?'

'That's what you say, that's the argument I've given myself too, but the fact is that I am a doctor on your mother's case. That's how you met me. It wouldn't be fair.'

'Is this fair?'

'Probably not, I probably shouldn't see you at all, or anyone like you, but I do a lot of things I probably shouldn't do.'

'I'm glad you do,' Kate said. She drew back and they smiled at each other. She wanted to take care of him; she knew he would take care of her.

'Come on,' he said, 'you've spent enough time in doctors' offices.'

'But it's fascinating,' Kate was reluctant to leave. 'What's all this?' She pointed to a low shelf where piles of paper covered with columns of numbers and hieroglyphs lay against a pile of copies of the *New England Journal of Medicine*.

'Oh, this is pretty boring, you really want to know?' Kate nodded.

'It's a study on the effects of dosage on breast cancer chemotherapy. Here are the figures for high doses given over a short period of time,' he ran a square finger over one column of numbers, 'and these are the figures for low doses over a longer period.' Riley hitched himself up on the desk and leaned forward. The wariness Kate had felt when they kissed was gone, now he was boyish and enthusiastic. 'We're using Cytoxan, methotrexate, and 5 F.U. Eventually all the patients get the same amount, it's a study about how it's administered. The first group of patients had five treatments in five months and the second ten in ten.'

'How did you decide that?'

'Meetings,' Riley laughed, 'everything here is decided at meetings.'

'Which dosage turned out to be better?'

'We don't know yet, it's a three-year trial. In the first year, it looked as if the high doses were working better, and that was pretty exciting. I wanted to switch everyone to high doses, but of course we don't operate that way, anyway now we're in the second year, and it's leveling off. It looks as if the disease responds to the actual amount of drugs, not the protocol schedule.'

'Was Dorothy Clay in the study?'

'At first she was in the high-dose group, but she dropped out pretty early, before she went down to Mexico.'

'She dropped out? It doesn't sound like her.'

'Her white-cell count was a problem. It's kind of self-defeating the way we treat cancer. We destroy as much as we can, and we hope we destroy the malignant cells. The drugs suppressed her immune system, so now we can't give her any more drugs. I hate this disease.' He said this quietly and bitterly, as if he were talking to himself. When he looked up, his expression made her feel closer to him than when they had been hugging and kissing.

'But you work here,' she said.

'Things were different when I started. Cancer was the great adversary, and we were winning. The government gave money, the Rockefellers gave money, remember Nixon's war on cancer?'

'It's still a worthy adversary, no?'

'Too worthy an adversary.'

'Come on!'

'I see a lot of patients, forty or fifty a day sometimes, and I might talk to twenty on the phone. Maybe I can help about thirty percent. They don't know that, but I do – and I'm working in one of the most successful treatment areas, it's much worse in neurology or colo-rectal.'

'I thought it was fifty percent, I thought fifty percent of cancer patients survived, that's what the newspapers say.'

'That's the statistic they use, but that counts a lot of very minor illnesses, skin cancers and such. By the time people get here, it's a lot less than fifty percent. Another thing about those statistics is that anyone who survives for five years is defined as cured. A patient can die in the sixth year and be cured and dead at the same time.'

'But this is one of the successful treatments?'

'Breast cancer is relatively responsive to drugs, in some cases, after surgery, say, the drugs can cut the recurrence rate from eighty percent to fifty percent.'

'That's doubling the chances!'

'Yes.'

'What about Ann's mother?'

'That's the thing, so many times it doesn't work.' Riley hopped off the desk and leaned against the filing cabinet now. Suddenly he looked very tired. 'People get here late, their doctors have told them it's nothing to worry about, or they don't go to the doctor at first because they're scared. No one wants to get this disease, and so they ignore the symptoms, and no doctors want to diagnose this disease, and so *they* ignore the symptoms. Once the get here, it's too late, or they don't respond well, things go wrong.'

'Are these treatments worth it, then? If they help so few people?'

'That's a good question, and it's one we don't ask enough

around here. With breast cancer, yes, often it is worth it, that's what makes this job bearable. But it's hard to deny treatment, even if you don't think it will help. They all want treatment; it gives them something to hope for. You can tell them that the drugs are experimental, and that no one knows if it works and that there are significant side effects, and they still want it. People have this incredible will to live, they'll do anything. I never realized how strong it was before I came here.'

'Do they ever ask you about suicide? I mean, about how they could do it, what pills they would need, or for a prescription?'

'Maybe twice in ten years, and never for a prescription. It's odd, because I think that's what I'd do. There are plenty of cases where . . . take your father for instance, by the time he got here, the chances that the drugs could help were quite small.'

'How small?'

'Well, maybe two or three percent . . . very small.'

Kate remembered her father's first examination and consultation at the hospital. The doctor had been all progress, all constructive suggestions, all recommendations about what could be done. He would never answer any questions about percentages, but he said that Gideon Loomis had a chance, a good chance, maybe even a very good chance.

That information had kept her father's spirit alive. That information had buoyed them all through agony, through illness, through humiliation. That information had kept them all going. That information had been false.

· 35 ·

Mack Riley took Kate's arm to guide her through the lunchtime crowds on Second Avenue. She leaned into him as they crossed 86th Street. The sun beat down on her shoulders and head.

'It's still so hot!' she said, but Riley didn't seem to hear her.

'I asked Ann to join us,' he said, 'she probably won't be there yet, she's always late.' But to Kate's chagrin there she was, standing in front of a restaurant awning in perfectly fitted, perfectly pressed slacks and a blue linen blouse. Riley led them both into the dark interior where plastic grapes hung from the ceiling, the walls were covered with shawls and maps of Spain, and each table had a wine bottle with a candle stuck in it for light. Ann slid into a booth near the bar and Kate sat next to her. Above them a gaudy gold and hot pink toreador's jacket hung from the stucco wall.

As Kate looked at the menu, which seemed to be mostly paella, she felt Riley looking at her. She tried to compose her face, to look happy. There were rules for getting along with men, Kate knew. Rules which should be remembered even when, or especially when, they invited another woman to an intimate lunch. For a minute she tried to convince herself that he had invited Ann because he was afraid to be alone with Kate, afraid of his feelings for her. That didn't work. Then she thought perhaps he had invited Ann because he wanted to see Ann so much that he didn't think about Kate. That didn't seem right either. Probably he just didn't think, except to imagine that two admiring, attractive women would be even more pleasant than one admiring, attractive woman.

'Paella,' she said, 'that sounds good.' Be positive, don't show jealousy – those were some of the rules.

'This place is nice,' Ann said, 'really, it reminds me of a waterfront café where we used to go in Barcelona.' She pronounced the soft *c* as a *th*. Kate thought this was affected, but Riley smiled at her.

'God, Ann how many languages do you speak?' he asked.

'Oh, I don't speak them, I just wheel and deal in them,' she said.

'I'm glad you're both here,' Riley said.

'I'm sorry I kept you so long in your office,' Kate said. She wanted to let Ann know that she and Riley had spent some of the morning together. 'It's just that it's so fascinating. I know you don't have a lot of time.'

'You two take a lot of time,' he said.

'It doesn't seem like much,' Kate said, smiling to show that she didn't mind being coupled with Ann, although she did. Another rule was not to complain.

He laughed, clearly enjoying himself. 'I would agree with that,' he said. Kate wanted to know how much time she was taking and how much time Ann was taking, but she didn't ask. That was against the rules. Kate knew that men liked to talk about themselves and their own problems. They didn't want women to have problems. As Ann and Riley chattered about Spain, Kate reflected that she had learned all these rules in order to be loved. That was the main thing. She had done this with David during their courtship, pretending to be entirely lighthearted, hiding her own real feelings under a veneer of cooperation just reluctant enough so that it felt like victory to him when she gave in. Later, when she couldn't hide her feelings, her frustrations about work, her fears, her grief over her father's death, later David wondered what on earth had changed her. She hadn't changed, she had just stopped acting. That was the trouble. Being loved was important, but it wasn't worth much unless it was someone you loved back. She didn't think about that though, until it was too late.

'It's amazing how much you've traveled, considering how little time you have,' she said to Riley, interrupting his conversation with Ann. Their talk sounded banal, but was he flirting with Ann with his eyes? or playing footsie with her under the table? Her compliment worked, and he turned toward her. Focus on the man and his achievements, that was a big rule. Act as if he were the only man in the world, a creature fascinating in his uniqueness. Kate felt Ann watching her too. They had a lot to say to each other, but the presence of Riley interrupted the flow of feeling and conversation between them.

'I do travel a lot, but I never get to stay anywhere long enough,' he said. Both Ann and Kate listened intently, as if he were saying something important. 'Usually I'm only in a place a week or less.'

'Do you go for conferences? or how does it work?' Kate asked. Riley was looking at her, but she couldn't get the possibility out of her head that he and Ann were touching each other under the table. She inched her own foot to the left toward Ann and encountered the table base.

'It's usually patients I've treated here, they call and ask me to come down. They're really just house calls. I spent a week in Hong Kong that way, a weekend in South Africa. Every now and then the State Department will send one of us somewhere on some kind of semisecret trip too, to treat an ambassador or someone who might be a spy.'

'Really, your job is so exciting!' Kate said. It was amazing how lame a statement could be if it was flattering. Their dishes of paella arrived, and Kate tasted the gluey rice and shrimp heavily seasoned with saffron.

'This is great,' Riley said, eating his with relish, 'I love Spanish food. My job is exciting,' he turned to Kate, 'but it has its downside too. You know what Shaw says in *The Doctor's Dilemma*, physicians are famous for the patients who die under their care. "A death advertises the doctor."' Their feminine attention seemed to make Riley voluble. Kate wondered if Ann was thinking about her mother, but she seemed to be laughing at Riley's wit along with Kate. Now she excused herself to make a telephone call.

'Now that we're alone, let's talk about us,' Kate said, lowering her voice into an imitation of a sultry come-on to show that this was a joke. It was important to be funny with men, to bring up the most serious things in a way that made them sound not so serious. Kate had learned to dance and skip at the edge of real meaning, never pausing long enough to let the man feel that she was too intent, too urgent. Riley smiled and reached across the table for Kate's hand. Suddenly he stopped smiling, and he seemed a moment away from some plunge into real seriousness. He seemed ready to confide, to say something that might change their friendship, or define it in a way that would push them forward. Maybe he would say that he wished they were alone, without Ann. Maybe he would suggest that they say goodbye to Ann and go back to his apartment after lunch.

'You're such a romantic creature, Kate,' he said.

'That's easy in this situation,' she said. He slid his hand off hers and beamed up at Ann as she sat back down.

'Everything all right?' he asked her.

'Lawyers!' Ann rolled her eyes in exasperation. 'At this rate I'm going to have to hire lawyers to handle my laywers.'

'A businesswoman, a writer, and a doctor,' Riley said. He had finished his paella and pushed his plate away with a look of satisfaction. 'We have a lot to teach each other.'

'How did you get into treating cancer patients anyway?' Ann asked him. 'I never asked you, what made you want to be an oncologist.'

'I always knew I wanted to be a doctor,' Riley leaned back and folded his hands in front of him. It was clear that he relished the question. Kate wished she had asked it. 'I don't know why I did. I guess it combined a position of respect and financial independence and being able to help people.'

'But why oncology?' Kate asked.

'I was going to be a pediatrician at first, but I got interested in oncology at Cornell. There was a group of us there, poor kids who didn't really fit in. We were anxious to be smart, to show up our professors. A few of us figured out that the one area where they didn't know very much was the area of cancer treatment. Their methods back then were pretty terrible. No one knew much about chemotherapy, so I made it my business to learn.'

'It was just rebelliousness?' Ann asked.

'Fifteen years ago, no one knew quite what to do with cancer patients; they were basically being left to die. When I get discouraged now, I try and remember that. Chemotherapy wasn't taken seriously then even when it worked.' Riley's face was animated as he talked. He forgot about the restaurant and the attentive faces of Ann and Kate. Men loved to talk about themselves.

'Ummmm hmmmm,' Kate said, nodding. That was usually all you had to do to keep them going.

'You've made a lot of progress,' Ann said. Kate slid out of the booth and headed toward the ladies room at the back of the restaurant. It seemed safe to leave them alone for a minute. The bathroom was dark with a tiny sink in the corner. Kate quickly combed her hair and powdered her face from her little blue compact. She gazed into her own deep, brown eyes in the mirror, fluffing her thick hair out with her fingers. Her skin looked luminous in the dim light. How could he resist her? Walking back to the table, she was relieved to see that Riley wasn't touching Ann as he had Kate when Ann left. They were still talking about chemotherapy.

'It was discovered by accident during World War Two,' Riley said. 'Let's get some coffee. There was an explosion in Naples harbor on a ship carrying some gas for secret warfare programs. The sailors had to swim in through the gas, which had an alkylating agent in it. Doing autopsies on the sailors, they discovered lymphoid and marrow hypoplasia which can cause remissions in lymphoma and some other types of cancer. The gas warfare project was top secret though, and it took them a while to understand what they had found.'

'And now?' Kate asked.

Riley blew on the surface of his coffee, the brown liquid had slopped into the saucer. 'Now chemotherapy is very sophisticated, and it really does work in certain areas, even the surgeons have to admit that. When I started, most people thought that if the malignancy couldn't be removed surgically, it was curtains. They compared chemotherapy to the leeches that doctors used to use for bleeding people. For some reason, I saw the opportunities.'

'You were smart, that's what,' Ann said.

'Lucky is more like it,' but Riley was obviously pleased. He poured the coffee from his saucer back into the cup and took a sip.

'You know I've been meaning to ask you,' Kate said. 'That first day when you explained things to me in the examining room, remember? There was a wonderful black cowboy hat sitting on the filing cabinet. Do you ever wear it? Don't you think he'd look great in a cowboy hat?' she asked turning to Ann.

'Oh no, I'm too conventional for that,' Riley said, as he signaled the waiter for the check. 'That's Lou Sander's hat, he just left it there, he's a real westerner. I can't imagine wearing a hat like that.'

· 36 ·

When they got to the corner, Ann kissed both Riley and Kate on the cheek and hailed a cab. Riley turned to walk downtown toward the hospital and Kate followed him. It was September, but the air was still hot and oppressive. As they crossed Second Avenue, Kate heard a distant roll of thunder and the sky over the buildings seemed to darken.

'It looks as if it's going to rain,' she said, 'maybe that will cool things off.' Riley didn't answer, but reached out and squeezed her shoulder. When she looked up, he was smiling over at her. 'But it's not raining now,' he said. He slowed his walk and kept his hand on her shoulder. Kate noticed that his face was flushed; he had drunk three glasses of Spanish wine with his paella.

'So are you going back to clinic?' she asked.

'Clinic got canceled this afternoon because of meetings,' he said. 'Somehow I'm having too good a time. I just don't feel like going back to work.'

'I don't blame you,' Kate said, she grinned up at him. 'Let's take a walk.'

'Katie!' Now Riley slid his hand across her shoulders and around the back of her neck, she felt her scalp prickle in response. 'You are a temptress.' He had stopped at the corner of Third. Behind him through the windows of a florist shop, Kate saw the bright pinks and yellows of summer flowers.

'We could go to the park, we could go up to my studio. What's a couple of hours on a summer afternoon?' she said. The thunder rolled again, this time it seemed to be coming from the river. 'Let's get out of the heat, at least.' She stood as close to him as she could without touching.

'Well, it is hot.'

'Come on then,' Kate tucked her arm through Riley's and turned him to the west. He moved with her. There were patches of blue sky to the east, but ahead of them a massive, black cloud bank hung over the buildings and towers of Lenox Hill.

'You know I shouldn't be doing this,' he said. He pressed her hand against his body with his arm.

'Every now and then people do things they aren't supposed to,' Kate said. 'It's not a big deal, it's called being human.'

'You have more opinions than anyone I've ever met,' he said.

'Is that bad?'

'No, I like it.'

'Well, that's something.' Kate was relieved to see that the doorman at her building was on his break. She opened the front door with her key and led Riley through the lobby.

'It's not the only thing I like,' he said. Kate pushed the elevator button for the top of the building. She had a twinge of guilt as they sped past the tenth floor where she lived with David, but she reminded herself that that was silly, because David wasn't even there. She let them into her office, turning the key in the lock and pushing open the door with her shoulder.

'I saw your office this morning,' she said, 'now you get to see mine.' Riley stood inside the door and looked around.

'It's nice,' he said, 'not what I expected.'

'What do you mean?' Out of the window she could see the rain clouds building up behind the water towers and cupolas in the west.

'It's cozier than I thought it would be, it doesn't look very officelike.'

'A woman's touch, you know,' Kate joked. He turned toward her.

'A woman's touch?' He reached over and picked up her hand. 'That's nice.' Kate felt a jolt of sexual current pass between them. He opened his hand palm up, fingers spread and laced them through hers in an embrace. Warmth seemed to flow from their hands through her body.

'I'm glad,' she said. Her voice sounded throaty and unfamiliar.

'You're blushing, Kate.' Riley moved toward her and cupped her cheek with his other hand. 'Your face feels hot,' he said.

Kate leaned forward into Riley's kiss. He slid his tongue around the edge of her lips and then pushed it deep into her mouth as he pressed his body against her. She slid her hand under his blazer, his shirt felt cool and smooth. His free hand caressed her neck and shoulders and then her breasts. She felt as if she was melting, as if her body was becoming part of his. His smooth supple hands seemed to be everywhere, stroking her back and lifting her skirt to part her thighs. Kate stepped backward toward the daybed, and Riley kept his body against hers. Every movement affected her physically, heightening her anticipation. The world fell away. Kate's whole being was concentrated on her body's pleasure in Riley, in the slight smell of soap on his skin, the feel of his wiry hair under her hands, and his mouth against hers.

'I want you,' he said, sliding her skirt up around her waist. This time, Kate let him unbutton her blouse and lay her on the daybed. Thunder rolled again in the distance, and she saw a flash of lightning at the windows. Riley stood to unbuckle his belt and let his pants fall to the floor. He knelt beside her undressing her and stroking her at the same time until she twisted and moaned with pleasure. He kissed her hair, her neck, her breasts and belly, the insides of her thighs. They didn't speak.

Afterward they lay entangled on the narrow couch. Riley's eyes were closed, he adjusted an arm under her head and kissed her shoulder. Kate floated in a honeyed cloud a few feet above her body. For a moment there was silence and absolute peace. Then there was thunder again, and she heard the sound of the rain splashing against the windows of the room, and the rain falling on the tar paper of the roof outside.

· 37 ·

'It's a good piece, but it's not exactly right for us, as it turns out,' Jeff Gordon said. He leaned back in his Naugahyde office chair and stared out the window at the office buildings on the other side of Madison Avenue. Light glinted off his aviator glasses and gave his smooth black hair a greasy sheen. Kate sat opposite him in a straight, wooden chair that reminded her of school. She looked right at Jeff Gordon, but her mind was soaring over his head, out the window, into the future. Less than twenty-four hours ago she had been rolling in Mack Riley's arms. She had felt the warmth of his loving and she still glowed. 'It's nicely written, you write very well, Kate, but none of us here is sure the artist merits this much space.'

'We talked about that before I started, Jeff.' Kate kept her voice friendly and a little flirtatious. That patronizing son of a bitch, she thought. Why am I sitting here listening to him when I could be reveling in my memories of yesterday. Gordon was an aggressive young editor, who liked to think of himself as irresistible to women. No one liked him much. Kate remembered a story someone had told her about Gordon being introduced to a young woman writer, and saying, 'Oh yes, didn't I sleep with you last summer?' and the young writer answering, 'Gee, I don't remember.' Everyone had laughed. Now Kate smiled, she knew that editors didn't like troublesome writers, and angry writers didn't get assignments.

'Yes, well, perhaps I didn't make it as clear as it could have been. I should have listened more carefully,' he said. It was easy for him to take some of the blame; he hadn't spent a month writing a piece that would not be published. 'We have another story for you, and of course you'll get the kill fee for this one. Bob wants to do a story on Picasso as an industry – all the different ways his art has been disseminated and exploited.'

'Okay, that sounds okay. Do you have any ideas about where to start?' Last time the kill fee had been seventy-five dollars. Kate had restrained herself from returning it with a rude letter.

'I've got some numbers for you,' Jeff said. 'Why don't you do a memo for us first, so we won't have this kind of misunderstanding again.'

It hadn't been a misunderstanding at all, and asking for a memo was just wanting more free work. If they decided not to proceed on the basis of the memo, she wouldn't get paid for the memo, of course. They had changed their minds, and they would change their minds again because they had nothing to lose. Kate could tell that Jeff Gordon was about to ask her out to lunch, and she got ready to turn him down. Men! They were mostly such fools. Jeff who thought he could jerk her around professionally and then feel her up under some white linen tablecloth. David who was never there when she needed him and who never noticed anything. She was in love with another man, and David's obliviousness was undisturbed. He probably wouldn't even notice if she didn't come home at night, if she moved Macklin Riley in and put his clothes in the closet! Mack Riley was the exception, because she loved him. Kate let the delicious heat of her feelings envelop her. She didn't want to have lunch with Jeff Gordon anyway, because she had promised David she would drop in on him, and she wanted to be back in her office by late this afternoon. Mack might call.

This office, Jeff Gordon, and her old life seemed unreal and insignificant next to the events of the summer, her mother's illness, and Mack. How could she ever have thought that this magazine office was an important place? That Jeff was an important man? What would Jeff Gordon say, she wondered,

· 163 ·

when he heard that she had left David and run off with her mother's oncologist? The asshole probably didn't even know what an oncologist was!

'How about some lunch,' Jeff Gordon leaned forward over his desk with a leer.

'I'd really like to, Jeff, but . . .'

'You're not sore about the piece, I hope?'

'Oh no, of course not, those things happen,' Kate laughed. 'It's just that I promised David I'd meet him at his office after this.'

'All right, Mrs. Weiss,' Jeff placed an unctuous emphasis on the Mrs. in her name. 'I'll take a rain check.' Kate left the white-brick office building. In the lobby a man with his head wrapped in gray rags rattled a tin can threateningly at everyone who came in and out. A uniformed guard stared at him but did nothing. As she stepped outside, a blast of late summer heat pushed her backward. The last thing she felt like doing was research on some aspect of Picasso. She wanted to write about art, not commerce.

The sidewalks were crowded with lunchtime groups, businessmen discussing this or that merger, gaggles of shopgirls and prides of laywers striding toward their reservations at expensive restaurants. Kate shouldered her way past the back of St. Patrick's and past Saks and into the cool, brass and marble lobby of David's building.

· 38 ·

'Mr. Weiss will be with you in a moment, will you have a seat?' Kate sank into the yellow silk loveseat which was part of the rich colonial decor in David's waiting-room. She wished Mack Riley could see her here, and be impressed. It was a new secretary, someone who obviously didn't know that Kate was Mrs. David Weiss, or that her father, Gideon Loomis, had been one of the founding partners. Kate looked up at the Audubon prints over the sideboard and decided not to make a fuss. She was tired, and anyway, she heard David's voice in the hallway now saying goodbye to a client. There was a low familiar murmur, and then a giggle, and then more of David's deep voice. It was a long goodbye. Finally the voices stopped, and one of the prettiest women Kate had ever seen – tall with startling green eyes and long wavy hair – walked down the hall from her husband's office. A phone on the secretary's desk buzzed and she picked it up.

'Mr. Weiss will see you now,' she said.

'Who on earth was that?' Kate asked, as she settled into one of the comfortable chairs behind David's desk. The scent of expensive, flowery perfume lingered behind the beautiful client.

'Oh, Cathy Brown, the widow Brown. She's an interesting case, she married Max Brown, I don't know if you remember, the pharmaceutical fortune. He died of a heart attack about a year ago leaving everything to her, and now the will is being contested. She'll be rich either way.' David leaned back in his chair. 'I really shouldn't take on this trust and estate stuff, but I made an exception.'

'I can see why,' Kate said.

'It's true, she doesn't want to work with anyone else, it was do it or lose a client.' David looked absurdly pleased with himself. He leaned forward toward her now in front of the big windows. Behind him she could see the skyscrapers of midtown falling away to the Hudson and the cliffs of Jersey on the other side of the river. Suddenly she saw her husband through another woman's eyes. He was handsome, charming, successful. The office was big and spoke quietly of David's successes with degrees, awards, and pictures of David with Senator-this and Congressman-that and even a President hung on the wall. David's manner was perfect, friendly but restrained, as if he were willing to help but would never impose, never go beyond the limits set by a client. The widow Brown must have been impressed.

'She probably wants to do more than work with you,' Kate said. She imagined the widow Brown with her luminous pre-Raphaelite looks, leaning toward David over a lunch table, inviting David up to her apartment to talk over her case.

'Maybe she does.' David shrugged and scanned the messages next to the telephone. He had lost interest in the subject. 'Senator Bullmore called again,' he said, 'wasn't he a friend of your father's?'

'Un unnh, and would you respond, I mean it must be tempting?'

'Hunh? Oh, come on, you know me better than that,' David said. He spoke confidently, not even bothering to look up at her. 'What's the point of being an ethics lawyer if you don't have any.'

'Still you admit, she's tempting.'

'A lot of things are tempting, especially in this business, especially right now because the code of acceptable behaviour has changed so much. But I'd have to be a real jerk to get mixed up with my clients, now wouldn't I? Anyway what about you, can I take you out to lunch, or are you just down here to see the dreadful Jeff Gordon?'

'Lunch,' Kate said. She had planned to hurry back uptown, but now she wanted to stay and be part of David's world. Mack had clinic until about four anyway, and he probably wouldn't call before then. If he did, well, it wouldn't hurt to let him know she wasn't always there waiting for him. Sunlight streamed through the wide windows onto David's partner's desk and comfortable leather chairs. Two walls were filled with books, a mixture of law and history, and the awards, degrees, and photographs were on the back wall where they were in view but not ostentatious. Her own likeness, in a silver frame, sat propped on the bookcase next to a leather box from Florence. She was glad to see her photograph there.

'How about Gino's?' David said. In his office he seemed quite different. Kate hadn't been down here since her mother got sick. Too busy; too angry. Here, she noticed, he had a kind of ease and competence that was not evident at home. He didn't dither or defer to her. He made decisions; other people carried them out. Kate nodded.

'Gino's one o'clock,' David told his secretary through the intercom. 'Tell Senator Bullmore I'll call him this afternoon.'

Kate felt pleasantly cared for as David ushered her down the hall into the elevators. All this was hers, and she had forgotten about it. Gino's was crowded, but the headwaiter recognized David and showed them to a banquette in the corner.

'Wine?' David said. 'So what happened with Gordon?'

Kate told him.

'Well, sweetie, that's how they're going to treat you as long as you free-lance,' he said. 'You could do anything, but they don't have any obligation to you as a free-lancer. What do you want to eat?'

'You order for me,' Kate said. David had just said what she expected him to say, but somehow it didn't sound that bad.

· 39 ·

Dr. Riley nodded to the security guard at the entrance and ran up the escalator past the information desk to the elevator banks. It was past five o'clock, he was late again. He had missed another department conference, but it probably wouldn't be noticed, except by old eagle-eyed Mallory. Still, he had spent too much time away from the office lately. Riley felt anxious when his life was unbalanced, when the ratio of play to work seemed upset. Lately he knew he had been playing a lot.

In the hall upstairs he ran into Bob Swords who wanted to piss and moan about the trouble he was having getting interleukin-2 for his patients. Riley didn't have trouble getting the drug for patients. He had made friends with Luke Ganz, the guy who ran the lab where it was being produced, but he didn't say anything about this to Bob Swords. That wasn't how it was done. Instead he murmured sympathetic agreement about the difficulties the older doctor was having. He valued his friendship with Swords, an old-fashioned doctor who had been at the hospital since the early days. Swords had gone to Yale in the great days of Dean Winternitz, and he read Yeats and Joyce and had sepia-tinted portraits of Joyce, Freud, and O'Casey on the walls of his office. He smoked a pipe and looked like an Oxford don. Riley treasured the old fellows, the doctors from a time when patient care – which Riley was good at – was valued far above research – which Riley was not good at. Swords had made great contributions, but his research was already out of date. As they spoke, his curved, wooden pipe puffed clouds of thick, aromatic smoke.

Riley was always surprised at how many of his colleagues smoked cigarettes or pipes. They all knew that respiratory cancers were caused by smoking. They had all seen lung cancer patients dying in terrible gasping agonies, but they didn't seem to notice. The doctors' lounges were always filled with smoke.

Cancer doctors, Riley knew, often had cancer symptoms. He had had a few: a lump in the groin that he thought was Hodgkins and turned out to be nothing, and an odd mole on his back. Most of the doctors who worked with cancer found themselves eventually having pains and problems which they could explain in only one way – the way they explained other people's problems day in and day out. Some doctors just ignored the symptoms, or joked about them, as if treating them irreverently would decrease their risk. They stayed too busy to worry. When it turned out that they didn't have cancer, that they had been right to ignore the symptoms, they began to feel invincible. It wasn't happening to them, and it wouldn't happen to them. They came to feel special, protected, not like other men and women, and exempt from the laws that governed them.

Other doctors became severely paranoid. Everyone around them had cancer – therefore it was just a matter of time until they got it. They took elaborate precautions. Some practiced holding their breath, so that they could refrain from breathing in heavy traffic or near truck or bus exhausts, others avoided sausage, or peanuts, or fried meats, or whatever foods had been implicated as carcinogens in the latest experiments. Of course, some oncologists actually did get cancer. Their colleagues treated them with surgery and radiation and chemotherapy. Their colleagues also treated them like freaks, aberrations in nature. Riley knew that it was terribly frightening to other doctors to see a doctor felled by the disease they had spent their lives trying to cure. They didn't like it, and they didn't like the sick man for reminding them that they were vulnerable. They were solicitous but distant. The doctor who had cancer became an outcast, and often suffered a psychological as well as a physical breakdown. Isolated by his colleagues, he knew too well what his chances were, he could imagine all too clearly his long, anxious journey to death. Suddenly he was thrown through the scrim of language, knowledge, and power which protects doctors from their patients. He could no longer protect himself by joking about the patients – he had become a patient.

On the way up the hallway to his office, before he went down to see Eddie Gomez, Riley ran into one of these men – these haggard reminders that no one is safe. It was Ed Lessons, Dr. Edward Lessons, a doctor who had been the head of a department, a great teacher, a beloved fellow. A year ago Riley and Lessons would stride down the hall together discussing patients and treatments. Now Lessons had lung cancer. He had been relieved of his duties at the hospital, but he kept his office. Mallory had operated on him, but the tumors had already been too large to resect. He was being treated in Riley's deparment with chemotherapy, massive doses which attacked the body and did not seem to be shrinking the tumors.

Everyone wished Ed Lessons would stay home, but he came to the hospital every day for as long as he could. His wife probably didn't want him at home any more than they wanted him at work. Now he shuffled slowly and painfully down the hall that had once been his kingdom. His head sagged downward, his hair was mostly gone, his clothes hung away from his body, his pants bunched around the waist where his belt had been tightened three extra notches.

'Riley,' Lessons whispered, fastening his glittering eye on Riley as he reached his office door. Lessons reached out and rested his bony hand on the younger doctor's arm.

'Edward, how are you feeling?' Riley said with pretended heartiness – how he was feeling was all too obvious. Riley was afraid that Lessons would come into his office and collapse on the couch. There was a time when Riley was pleased to have Ed Lessons drop by his office.

'It's terrible,' Lessons said, 'terrible, I had no idea.' He sounded like the last survivor of some awful battle or shipwreck. Riley felt impatient. Most of the doctors wouldn't even stop to talk with Ed Lessons. he had a lot of things to do today. Lesson's voice croaked, and he spoke slowly as if he had to press each syllable out of his chest.

'You don't know,' Lessons said. Riley flinched at this honesty and involuntarily stepped backward, throwing Lessons off balance. It looked as if he might fall, and Riley quickly took his arm.

'These treatments,' Lessons croaked, 'these treatments are terrible. I think we underestimate our patients, we don't know what we're doing to them.' Riley was stung. Lessons, his old colleague, was talking about treatments Riley administered every day, that he and Riley had administered together. Riley prided himself on his compassion for his patients.

'I think I know what my patients are going through,' he said in spite of himself. What on earth was the use of arguing with this sick old man?

'Maybe you do.' Now Lessons looked up at Riley knowingly as if he had some message to give. His frailty and desperation made his old friend seem suddenly gnomic and sinister. 'Be careful, Mack,' he said.

'What do you mean?' With relief, Riley saw that he had been able to deter Lessons from entering his office, and he pointed the other man firmly toward the elevator banks.

'It's something I heard,' Lessons was speaking faster now, and the malevolence in his gaunt face was unmistakable. 'They didn't know I was listening, I hear everything now,' he said. He straightened his body slightly, let go of Riley's arm, and shuffled off down the hall.

Riley stepped into his own office and shut the door. He felt shaken. What had Lessons heard? What should he be careful of? He should have invited the older man into his office and found out, but he couldn't do it, he just couldn't do it. There was a stack of fresh messages on his desk, and the phones were ringing. It was too late to go down and see Eddie now. He answered one phone and talked to Mrs. Rice, a fifty-four-year-old woman from Philadelphia who was coming for post-surgical adjuvant treatment. After that he felt better. There was too much to do to worry about Ed Lessons and his enigmatic warning. He was sick, Riley could make allowances for that. He was too sick to know what he was saying.

· 40 ·

Ann's oldest friend was a girl named Lisa, only she pronounced it Leeza. She and Ann met Kate for lunch about a week after Kate's afternoon with Mack Riley. Kate had spoken to Riley only once since then. After waiting for him to call her for two days, she had broken down and called him. He had been friendly and businesslike and preoccupied. He acted as if they were friends as they always had been, as if nothing had changed. Kate was eager to see Ann again. Because of their circumstances, being with Ann somehow made her feel close to Mack Riley, and Ann might drop some information about his whereabouts or his frame of mind.

The restaurant was crowded with women dressed for lunch, their streaked hair swept back in stiff manes, their small features emphasized with makeup. This was a world where men went to work in the morning and wives slept late, and then got dressed for lunch and did a little shopping before they went home and got dressed for dinner. Kate's hair was dark and long like a girl's, her nails blunt and unpolished.

Ann was wearing a soft gabardine suit. Her nails were shaped and painted like tiny pink shells. Lisa wore a black cotton sweater and a grimy trench coat, but she seemed perfectly relaxed as she lit a cigarette and leaned back in the wicker chair.

'So, Princess,' she said to Ann, 'what's the gossip? How's your life going?'

Ann cocked her impeccable head sideways and smiled. 'There's good news and bad news,' she said. She didn't seem to mind being called Princess.

'Let me guess,' Lisa said. 'You're not getting along with Scott.'

'Well, that's not news at all,' Ann countered.

'I have to admit, there are times when I feel for that poor guy,' Lisa said. 'Did he ever sign a prenuptial? Knowing your father, I don't even have to ask. What would happen to him if you dumped him, he'd have to go back to teaching tennis to rich girls?'

Kate was stunned by Lisa's manner, but Ann didn't seem to notice. 'I don't think he'd do that,' she said.

'Still, he's probably sick and tired of being just another tame vice president.'

'If he's tired of it, he can leave,' Ann said. She seemed irritated at Scott, not at Lisa. 'Are you and David coming out this weekend?' she asked Kate. They had arranged this a long time ago. Kate nodded. But Lisa did not want to change the subject.

'Poor bastard, I always liked him,' Lisa said.

'He may be available soon enough,' Ann said.

'So who's this doctor we're hearing so much about, Dr. General Hospital, Dr. Understanding?' Lisa asked. Kate's heart thumped and she let out an involuntary murmur. 'You know him too, right?' Lisa turned to her, 'This guy casts a wide net.'

'He's the doctor for both of our mothers,' Kate said, trying to keep her voice steady. 'It's an odd coincidence.'

'He's a lot more than that,' Lisa said. She was drinking black coffee with her salad. Kate and Ann drank soda water.

'He's been a great friend, he's been very helpful,' Ann said. She glanced up at Kate.

'That's not how you talked about him the last time I saw you, kiddo. He's the only one who understands you, he's the only one who knows what you're going through, blah, blah, blah,' Lisa said.

'Come on, Lisa,' Ann said, 'watch your mouth. Here's Scott's office number if you're so hot to commiserate with him.' She handed Lisa one of her heavy vellum cards with Scott's name and number written on the back.

'God, you've got great handwriting, Princess,' Lisa said as she took the card. 'I wish I'd learned that at school.'

'That's funny,' Ann looked calm and happy. She had eaten about half her salad, but she nodded to the waiter that she was finished. 'You're the second person who's told me this week that I have beautiful handwriting.' Something about the way Ann said this made Kate sure that the first person who had told her was Mack Riley. Kate felt confused. That wasn't so bad, was it, if he had complimented her on her handwriting? It could mean nothing. At dessert, Ann and Kate ordered decaffeinated coffee, and Lisa had chocolate cake with whipped cream. The sugar seemed to rile her up even further.

'I don't want to malign this doctor,' she said, 'I mean, I've never even met the guy, but there's something weird about this. I worry about you, Princess. You're so capable, but right now you're pretty vulnerable.'

'I wish you could understand,' Ann said, 'this doctor is a great man. He's helped Mummy a lot, and she adores him. It would have been a nightmare without him.'

'Is he helping you, or are you helping him?' Lisa demanded. 'Christ, the way you fawn over him, it's enough to make me think about going to medical school.'

'Lisa,' Ann protested. The cake was gone, the whipped cream scraped clean.

'He's a very unusual man,' Kate said. 'A lot of doctors are practically inhuman, they treat everyone just like another case. Riley is compassionate, he cares about his patients.'

'Compassionate, come on! Messing around with patients' families isn't caring for the patients. It's not a fair situation, everyone knows that, for God's sake.'

Kate stared into her coffee cup. A sharp ache at the bottom of her stomach forced her to bend forward. Lisa was right. Rude but right. She looked across at Ann's place and saw that Ann's coffee cup was full. Ann was blushing and staring right at her. Kate looked away.

'Let's get the check and get out of here.'

Later Kate walked quickly away from the restaurant. She

wanted to leave the whole thing behind, the pain and the confusion. Obviously, something was going on between Mack Riley and Ann. Of course, she should have known that. But what? and what were his feelings about her? Kate let herself into the apartment and thumped down on Hilda's overstuffed sofa. It was cool and dark in the living room with the air-conditioning on and the shades drawn. Why did this have to happen? Why did it have to happen that when she finally fell in love with someone, there had to be another woman involved? Why did this messy, excruciating situation have to happen to her? Kate stared across the room at the mahogany table where David read in the evening. Something like this would never happen to David. For a moment Kate thought that perhaps this had happened to her because she had sought it out and let it happen. This was too much. She burst into tears and buried her head in the soft fabric of the couch.

· 41 ·

Ann and Scott Lacey lived in a white frame house in Greenwich near the Sound. Once the carriage house for the Clays' bigger house, which stood behind it in a grove of beeches, it had been remodeled when Ann had married, fifteen years after her parents had decided to establish a base in the northeast so that their only child could go to the proper schools. These days, Adam Clay was always away, and his wife was ill. But the two architecturally matched houses stood gleaming in the sun at the end of a long sweep of drive, flanked by bright flower beds and shaded by the maples and beeches, as serene as if nothing had happened since the family moved in. Ann was grateful that nothing had changed, but at the same time she was depressed by the heartlessness of wood and stone.

Scott Lacey, Ann's husband, was a tall man with a flop of yellow hair, a snub nose, and a line of freckles across his cheekbones. When he had met Ann Clay, she had been on vacation with her mother, and he was the tennis pro at the Camden Harbor Yacht Club. Now he was the vice president of her father's company, and she was his wife.

On an autumn afternoon, the stillness around the houses was ruptured by the sound of low voices and the regular thud of the tennis ball against a racket. Kate and David, Scott and Ann, were spending an afternoon at the Laceys'. Kate had been looking forward to meeting Scott Lacey, and at first she had found him quite bland and excessively polite. She was disappointed. Covertly she was rooting for Scott Lacey. The better his chances of staying married to Ann, the less chance there was that Ann would go after Mack Riley. But later, as she watched him play singles with David, she got a sense of frustration and power pent up in his lanky body. Scott had been a pro, of course, and his game was graceful and definitive, but Kate was pleased to see how well David was playing. She hadn't remembered how well he looked on a tennis court, trim in his whites, and she was proud of the way he returned Scott Lacey's shots. Scott's serves were strong and courteous, but occasionally he put all his weight behind the ball, and those had the force of lethal weapons. Kate wondered how Scott Lacey felt about being someone's pet vice president.

'Scott is a pleasure to watch,' she said. Ann didn't answer. 'Anyone who saw us here would think, "what nice-looking young people,"' she tried again.

'Nothing unusual, nothing unconventional,' Ann replied, but there was a bitterness in her tone. 'Nothing unusual at all.'

'How's your mother doing?' Kate asked. The four of them had gone through lunch on polite, banal commentary. No one had mentioned disease, or doctors, or any of the things they had in common.

'She's a lot worse actually,' Ann seemed relieved to be able to talk about her mother. 'Mack doesn't say that of course, but I can tell. The Mexican clinic was kind of a turning point, first she seemed to get much better, but now she's much worse. He's been a great support. I don't think we could have gone through it the way you did, all that waiting.'

'He's a very controlled character.' Kate thought of Mack on her daybed, abandoning himself to his pleasure in making love to her. Out of the corner of her eye, she saw David bring Scott up to the net and then lob a shot over his head to win the game. They returned to the baseline. Scott's serve.

'Repressed, isn't that what you mean? It's hard for him to know what he wants, to take what he wants.'

'Do you think he's available? I know he's separated from his wife, but he seems so remote, sexually I mean.' Kate probed for information. Scott was serving now, and David gave the ball a spin to the left. Scott missed the shot. His game was becoming wilder as the power on the court began to shift.

'Remote?' Ann Lacey seemed surprised at the word. 'I don't know. Ultimately, I guess I think he is available, I suppose everyone's available given the right conditions,' she said.

'He seems pretty tough,' Kate said, 'or frightened.' Now Scott barreled two serves across the net at David, who let them go.

'Oh Christ, I wish Scott would stop playing that way,' Ann said. 'He can't learn to be civilized.'

'He plays wonderfully,' Kate said.

'I know, but he hates to let anyone else win, I can understand that I suppose, there are just days when everything about him irritates me.'

'That may be a definition of marriage,' Kate said.

'Maybe, I don't really see why I should settle for that, frankly. There aren't any children, there isn't any reason to do what my parents did for me – even if they should have. I don't think this marriage will go on much longer at any rate,' Ann added. 'We're talking about a separation.'

'Why didn't you have children?' Now Scott was slamming his forehands across the court, playing a game of sheer strength which David couldn't withstand. Kate wished she could tell David how well he had done.

'A couple of miscarriages,' Ann shrugged. 'After that it didn't seem worth pursuing. What about you?'

'It was easy to put off. We decided against it, and then we started talking about it again, but then my father got sick, and now I guess I'm glad I stalled. A lot has happened.' Kate could see that Scott had won the set. David and Scott walked to the net and shook hands. David's face was flushed with health, and he smiled to show that he didn't mind losing. Even though he had won, Scott seemed to sulk. The two men turned toward the house and Kate could hear David asking the polite questions he was so good at.

'But you'd still want to have children?' Ann was asking.

Now Kate shrugged. 'That's a good question,' she said, 'I don't really know.' But suddenly she felt the impossibility of having children with David. He wasn't interested anyway. Her obsession with Riley had shifted her attention away from David and their marriage. Their apartment, their life together, their shared interests, all seemed faintly dreamlike, as if David were a handsome stranger in a book or a movie. At the same time, sitting on this manicured lawn, Kate had a sudden violent urge to have a child. To give birth to a baby who would return her love. To fill the void of human loneliness with another life. To take care of someone else, instead of worrying about who was going to take care of her. For the first time, she felt she was getting older, and she remembered Mack saying that putting off childbirth increased the risk of cancer.

'The south wing was added later in the century,' she could hear Scott telling David as he gestured toward the big house where Dorothy Clay lay in an upstairs bedroom. The two men were walking off the court now. 'You can see the different styles of the lintels, and the different kinds of columns on the new wing. Of course, we'll have to move over there and rent this one when . . .'

'Do you have to talk that way?' Ann interrupted him angrily.

'Sorry,' Scott said, but he didn't sound sorry. Kate could almost see his lower lip protruding in a little boy's pout.

The sun was low in the sky now, the days were getting shorter. The light and warmth of summer seemed to be disappearing behind the branches of the great beeches and privet hedges that bordered the Clay lawns. This was and would always be the summer that she had fallen in love with Macklin Riley. Kate stretched her legs out on the cool, velvety grass. It was September now, almost October. The leaves were turning red and gold on the big maples in front of Dorothy Clay's windows. The ground felt cold under her feet, the shadow of night was sharper, and Kate remembered that winter was coming. Soon the green rich lawn would be covered with snow, the great trees bent down by ice, their branches bare. Ann's mother might be dead by then, no longer looking out her windows at the sky, no longer visiting the hospital, no longer anything.

Kate thought of her own mother. At first the radiation treatments had not had any side effects, but later they had become very difficult. Matilda Loomis felt sick all the time. Her back began to hurt, her legs pained her, and she had trouble walking. Macklin Riley said this was normal. The doctors took X-rays and said it was nothing to worry about. Her father had had trouble walking, too. And now her mother . . .

Then Matilda Loomis had gone into the hospital for her radium implant. For three days she was confined to a hospital bed and not allowed to move. No one was allowed to visit her for more than three minutes because she was radioactive. There were danger signs and 'Do Not Enter' signs all over the door to her room. On the fourth day the doctors removed the radium implant and sent her home. She said she felt better. The doctors said she was fine. Kate didn't believe them.

· 42 ·

There was a system to Dr. Peter Mallory's clinic, but it didn't always work. As patients' names came up, the nurse would usher them from the hallway into the examining room. Mallory would take the patient's chart off the cart next to his secretary.

'How are you doing, Mr. Doe?' he would say cheerily, reading the name off the chart. Sometimes it would be the wrong name, the wrong chart, and they all sat there in uncomfortable silence as the nurse was sent to get the right one.

'Now,' Mallory would say, 'tell me why you are here,' or he would ask his questions, jotting the information down on a piece of paper. 'Do you smoke much?' 'Do you drink?' 'What symptoms made you see a doctor?'

Mallory had verbal formulas to deal with the awkwardness of the physical exam. 'Let's get you elegant,' he would say as he wrapped the flimsy gown around the patient's body. 'Now I'm going to take a stool sample,' he would say, in a tone of voice that made it clear the rectal exam was going to hurt, but that it was all right if it hurt. No one complained.

'Now, what else can we do for you?' he always said at the end of the exam, as if he had time to attend to the patient's every need, answer every question. The secret was an intensity of attention which allowed him to hurry from patient to patient, appearing to be totally interested in each case.

The visits went quickly. Mr. Oakes from Chicago had a melanoma that had metastasized in ugly black lumps across his chest. Mallory decided that he was a good candidate for an experimental program at the National Cancer Institute.

Professor Meger from Vermont had had a stomach tumor removed two years ago and was in for a follow-up, everything fine. Mrs. Hallas from Detroit brought in a CAT scan which showed a significant tumor in her right abdominal cavity.

After a few minutes of talk and questions, Mallory would gather up the patient's X-rays, records, and CAT scans, ask them to wait a minute, and hurry out of the office and down the hall to another room where he examined everything on a big light box. It was easy to spot the major tumors, asymmetrical gray masses pushing at the normal limits of the body or the internal organs. It was harder to tell if he would be able to remove them on the operating table. (Later, after clinic, he would take them downstairs and go over them again with other doctors and with the radiologist.)

Then, Mallory would return to the patient in the examining room. His manner was sympathetic and positive. He talked only about what could be done, not about what couldn't. As the patient left, often to make an appointment for surgery, he dictated a memo into his pocket tape recorder, and letters to other doctors on the case. The whole thing took about seven minutes.

There were two patients in clinic that afternoon who both probably faced losing a leg. One woman was in tears before Mallory walked into the examining room. Her husband and two sons stood stoically behind her. She had already been to another hospital where they told her that she had less than a ten percent chance of surviving. Mallory didn't talk about survival. Instead he examined the leg. A rash of black spots had appeared between the knee and the ankle over the scars where other spots had already been removed. He handled the flesh gently.

'In my opinion,' he said, 'this would be a case for perfusion. We pump a chemical into the blood system of the entire leg, and that should be followed with a wider excision of the melanoma. After that we can try treating it with monoclonal antibodies. We may have to think about losing the leg, but we may not.' The woman had stopped crying. Mallory's attitude was infectious. Something could be done.

'You sound a lot different than the other doctors I've talked to,' she said.

'I'm not changing the percentages,' Mallory warned, 'but I think there are things we can do here.'

'I don't care,' the woman said, 'I like it here.' The husband and sons smiled. Mallory had done it again.

The next patient was a small woman with harlequin glasses who was waiting in the examination room with her sister. She had gone to her doctor a year ago because she had a painful lump in her upper thigh. He had told her not to worry. Now Mallory had to tell her that she would probably lose the leg.

'This is not a minor problem,' he said, 'but it is not an acute problem.' An acute problem was death. Hearing the worst seemed to relieve this woman. She chewed her red lipstick and fiddled with her black pocketbook, but Mallory had defused her panic. Her sister patted her on the shoulder.

'I've been under a lot of pressure, doctor,' the woman said. 'I've been nursing my son, he was hurt in a mugging. It's cost a lot, we've had to move to a smaller apartment.' Mallory listened intently. He let her talk. He knew the real questions would come later. She was smiling when he finally left the room.

'I'm a psychiatrist,' he complained to the nurse as he passed in the hallway. 'A goddamned psychiatrist.' The woman with the harlequin glasses had taken half an hour on a morning when twenty-six patients had to be seen in four hours.

The next patient was a tan, dark-haired man with three pendants spread across the hair on his chest. Danny Rakes from Fort Lauderdale, Florida. Last New Year's Eve when Danny Rakes had been in the hospital, he had ordered two cases of champagne for the nurses. He was a legend with the staff, and he got a big welcome when his name was called.

Danny Rakes had a different attitude than most of Mallory's patients. He was intent on having a great time with the life he had left to him, partying and traveling while the tumors grew under his tanned flesh. When they grew too big he would have them out like he had had the other ones out. He was bursting with energy.

'How the hell are you, Doc?' he asked Mallory, as he was being examined.

'Fine, just fine, I don't feel anything unusual, let me have a look at the scans,' Mallory said.

'Life is for living,' Danny Rakes grinned. The scans showed that the tumors could be left alone for another three months.

'You're doing something right,' Mallory said.

'*We* are, Doc,' Danny Rakes reminded him. This time Mallory left the room smiling.

The next patient was a Mr. Padonna from California who had cancer of the pancreas. An Italian immigrant who listed his occupation as construction, Padonna had flown in from the coast with his wife and pretty daughter. The daughter's husband, a thin man with a pencil mustache, was a surgeon in San Diego. The parents hardly spoke English, but the pretty daughter had married a doctor, and their children would go to college. On the CAT scans, there was a tumor larger than a fist, a spot like an irregular ink spill on the film. Mallory told the Padonnas he would have to operate before he could tell what kind of tumor it was. He also explained that he might not be able to remove it.

'The operation is the next step,' he said. 'After that we'll have more to go on.'

'Our doctor at home sent us here,' the pretty daughter spoke; her head was bowed, and blonde hair hid her features. 'He said, well ... do you think it will be, you know ... terminal?'

'It may be a garden variety pancreatitis, or it may be a more virulent kind,' Mallory said, avoiding the question. 'We have no evidence of that now, we'll know more after we operate.' In cancer of the pancreas, more virulent means less than six months, garden variety means maybe a year, but Mallory didn't say that.

'Then we don't know, we can't make any plans,' the daughter said.

'No, no plans until we see.'

'Should we encourage him to eat? He's so thin,' she asked. Mr. Padonna had lost thirty pounds. Patients often asked Mallory about diet and bowel movements when they meant to ask questions about life and death. His answers were always about diet and bowel movements.

'Encourage him to eat, but don't be upset if he can't,' Mallory said. 'Let's make an appointment for him to come in and have the operation next week.' Padonna and his wife sat silently in the blue plastic chairs against the beige wall. They didn't ask questions, they didn't even seem to be listening. They had the ancient look of peasants sitting on the straw by a hayrick or on the front steps of a stucco farmhouse – a look as if their lives were beyond time.

'He's lost so much weight,' the daughter said. She looked up and put her long graceful arm around her father's bowed shoulders. 'If you could have seen him before this, Doctor, my father was such a strong man, he was the strongest man.' Her voice broke, and her blue eyes filled with tears, her fine skin flushed. 'I'm sorry,' she said, 'I'm sorry.'

'Don't be,' Mallory said gently. But Mr. Padonna, seeing his daughter's distress, had begun to cry too; tears ran down his weathered, expressionless face. It was something to cry about, this sudden destruction of a family's life, this interruption of a story by an arbitrary and brutal disease. It was all right, really. The daughter had married a successful and compassionate man, their children would go to college anyway. At that moment, though, it didn't seem all right. Mallory was up from the desk, and in a few seconds, really before the time it takes to have feelings, he was out the door and on to the next case.

Later, upstairs, Mallory ran into Mrs. Connors, a big blue-eyed woman who grabbed him and kissed him before he could avoid it.

'I can't believe it,' she said, 'you're a miracle worker, Doctor!'

'Well, I didn't quite make the schedule,' Mallory said.

'He's coming home, the kids are so excited,' Mrs. Connors kept touching Mallory as if he had some kind of totemic magic that might rub off on her.

'I'm very pleased,' Mallory said. Dan Connors was sitting up in bed with an almost empty dinner tray next to him. Since the operation he had been able to eat, and the feeling that he was getting better had revitalized his gallant spirit. Watching him now as he told his wife what to pack and made plans for his own homecoming, Mallory remembered the growing melanomas he had left inside Connors's gut, the ones he couldn't reach, and he pushed the thoughts away.

'Well, Dan, try not to be so sad about leaving us,' he said, laughing. Connors was scooping up the photographs of his children and pulling their drawings off the walls to take with him. None of them thought about him coming back, as he inevitably would, or about what it would mean if he didn't come back. Dan Connors had a terminal disease in its advanced stages, but right now, he was more alive than most people ever were. Mallory squeezed his shoulder, holding back an urge to cry himself, wished him well, and left the room.

· 43 ·

Macklin Riley had saved the best for last; all morning as clinic dragged on he had promised himself a visit to Eddie Gomez to tease him about the Mets. Lately the little boy had seemed better, enjoying one of those mysterious remissions that patients sometimes have. Kinsey had kept him in the hospital for observation, but his room had been a cheerful place filled with notes from his classmates at school, balloons, baseball paraphernalia, and visitors from his family and the hospital staff.

As Riley approached the nurses' station on the fifth floor, he noticed that Eddie's door was closed.

'Eddie's worse,' the dark-haired nurse said. 'He's been asking for you, he was up most of the night.'

Riley pulled Eddie's chart off the shelves and opened it to the last entries.

'Low white-blood-cell count has caused sluggishness and headaches. Patient quite depressed. Rx: morphine PRN,' said the first note last night, scrawled in almost illegible black ink and signed with an indecipherable signature that Riley knew belonged to David Kinsey – Eddie's attending physician.

'Eddie was up at four and asked me to call his mother and have her come in.' This note was written in the schoolgirl backhand of the head nurse. 'Morphine for sleep.'

Riley's heart pounded. There was no reason for Eddie to be worse, he had been diagnosed as having leukemia only six months before, and although the bone marrow transplant hadn't worked, this was only his second remission. As he walked quickly down the hall, he squared his shoulders. Eddie

Gomez was not going to get worse, he told himself. He was not going to let this happen.

He knocked and pushed open the door to the little boy's room.

'I came down to razz you about the Mets,' he said. Eddie lay in bed, with Tom Seaver's blue cap over his narrow chest. His head tossed on the pillow, he managed a wan smile. Riley noted that the IV was still feeding him morphine for the pain.

'C'mon, kiddo, you can't be blue, we need you to cheer the rest of us up,' Riley said. He walked over and lifted Eddie's wrist to take a pulse. Without counting he could feel that it was too slow.

'It just hurts,' Eddie said. It wasn't a complaint, just a statement of fact. He struggled to pull himself up to a sitting position, and Riley helped him, boosting him up against the pillows under the elbows. With every touch, Riley tried to sneak a little of his own health and energy into the kid's body.

'There now, that's better,' Riley said, perching himself on the edge of the bed. Eddie's body took up a sliver of space under the sheets, but he smiled more broadly.

'I asked for you,' he said, 'I wanted to give you something.'

'Probably a piece of your mind,' Riley joked. 'Listen, it wasn't my idea to be a Red Sox fan, I was born there, I didn't have any choice.'

'No, something else,' now Eddie was smiling as if he was enjoying a private joke. He lifted the treasured baseball cap off his chest and held it out to Mack Riley. 'This,' he said.

'You look better already,' Riley said. He pretended not to understand.

'Here,' Eddie said. He continued to hold the cap toward Riley.

'What?' Riley felt tears start up in his eyes. He looked down and composed himself. The little boy must not see that he was upset. He must not see it.

'I want you to have this,' Eddie said.

'You're kidding, that's your most precious goddamned possession, I wouldn't take that,' Riley said. But Eddie had let go of the cap over Riley's hands and he caught it as it fell to the bed.

'That's the point, idiot.'

'Come on, Eddie, I can't take that, what will your mother say, the nurses will think I'm a thief – taking a kid's treasure. They don't think that much of me anyway.'

Eddie just smiled. 'It's yours,' he said.

'What do you mean? I can't take it,' Riley tried to put the cap back on Eddie's head, but the little boy blocked him with an outstretched hand. 'Keep it,' he said.

'Okay, I'll keep it for you until you want it back,' Riley said. He was having trouble controlling his face.

'Yeah, that's good,' Eddie said. 'Keep it until I want it back.'

Riley took the cap, holding it folded in one of his big hands. The orange Mets insignia on the blue wool glowed vividly in the light from the room's window. Outside, the sun glinted off the swirls and eddies of the treacherous currents in the East River. It was a beautiful day.

'I'll keep it for you,' Riley said. His voice was even now, he had put off his feelings for later, or for never. That was what you did.

'Listen, Riley, it's nice of you to come down and see me, but don't you have other things to do around here?' Eddie slumped back down under the sheet. His black hair was damp with sweat across his forehead, his face pale again.

'Yeah,' Riley said, 'yeah, you're right, I have lots to do.' He stood up and smoothed the hair away from the boy's face. Then he leaned over and kissed Eddie's forehead, but the boy's eyes were already closing. The morphine. Riley stood for a moment, feeling numb and then turned to walk away.

'See ya,' Eddie's voice whispered behind him. Riley wheeled around, but Eddie's eyes were closed. He was already gone, drifting in the helpless sleep. His breath came in a long, shallow, irregular sequence. The monitors ticked next to his bed. The sun flashed off the metal sidebars. Far away in the city somewhere, Riley could hear horns honking and the distant, mournful toll of a bell.

· 44 ·

Kate sat on a cold stone bench in the court around the fountain at the Frick Collection. Waiting for Mack. Since that magical afternoon, which now seemed like a distant and golden moment, Kate had spoken to him three times on the telephone. He had been consistently friendly, preoccupied, and a little distant. Men get close, and then they back off. In her head, Kate knew that Mack was probably frightened and worried. She was married. She was the daughter of a patient. She was against the rules. In her heart she just hurt. His cool, friendly voice seemed to turn her to ice, ice which later melted into the cold pain in her guts. But she went along with it, echoing his reticence, his humor, his old pal manner with her. She had no choice. Every few minutes she got up and walked over to the entrance to the museum to see if he had arrived. It was October, still warm, with the acrid smell of fall in the air, and past the big french windows in the Fragonard Room, she could see the sunlight slanting into the red and yellow maple leaves in the park.

She hadn't been to the Frick in years, meeting there was Riley's idea, and after weeks of not seeing him, she would have been delighted to meet him anywhere he chose. When she was growing up though, the Frick had been her secret refuge, her home away from the home in the city. She would take the train into town, down the Hudson from Westchester, and walk up Madison Avenue from Grand Central to sit in the court at the Frick, waiting – waiting for her life to happen. Sometimes men would sit next to her on the stone bench and try to start conversations. Sometimes they carried books or had name tags from business conventions on their blue suits. There were never very many people at the Frick in those days.

Kate was always interested, at first. It seemed impossible to her that anyone could find her attractive enough to sit next to. But then she usually noticed something about these men – a weakness in the eyes, or a nervous tic, or too much eagerness, or cheap shoes – that made it easy to freeze up and say no, as if she had never even considered it.

It was at the Frick, one of those afternoons, that she had met Randall Bond. She was carrying a bunch of wild flowers from the country and a book of poetry, and her guitar was next to her on the floor. He was striding along contemplatively, his long arms behind his back, through the stone arches. A slender man with a narrow face, he had blue eyes and wore a soft tweed jacket, and as soon as Kate spotted him she wanted to make an impression. She knew right away that he would not be interested in her – men like that were not interested in her. She felt safe. She looked directly up at him as he passed, and he looked down and noticed her book. 'You're reading Philip Larkin?' he said, he had an English accent, 'what a remarkable choice for a young girl.' Later, she sat very close to him as he read from the book in a low, melodious voice, and held her hand under the table of a coffee shop on Madison Avenue.

> No I have never found
> The place where I could say
> This is my proper ground,
> Here I should stay;
> Nor met that special one
> Who has an instant claim
> On everything I own
> Down to my name . . .

He read in his delicious, authoritative accent. Kate's heart fluttered. She and Randall Bond were both nomads, children, both people who understood that the sweetness of each moment was nothing more than that.

When they left the museum for the coffee shop, Randall Bond had carried her guitar, and when he said he would love to hear her play and sing, it seemed perfectly all right to go back to his apartment with him. She was eighteen, she had been off crutches for two years, she was ready for an adventure.

Kate imagined a series of afternoons, in winter in the softly falling snow, in summer in the blazing heat. She would come in on the train, Randall Bond would meet her, and they would go to his apartment where she would play and he would listen and dream. They would have long talks and read poetry to each other. He would understand her as no one else did. She would tell him about her parents and the accident, and all her longings, and he would be gentle, attentive, and concerned. He would see the quick and loving Kate – the Kate who was temporarily trapped in a plump, crippled, postadolescent body. Randall Bond had told Kate that he was an actor. She would wait backstage for him, or sit in the audience reveling in her special connection to the dazzling Englishman on stage.

Randall Bond's apartment was in the basement of a brownstone on 67th Street off Third Avenue. He led Kate in through wrought-iron gates with a thespian flourish and unlocked a green metal door. Inside the apartment the air was hot and dark with a gamy, slightly sour smell. There were clothes scattered everywhere, and Randall Bond bent down to pick them up and stuff them in a closet.

'Excuse the mess,' he said, 'the maid comes tomorrow, now you sit down right here, and I'll get you a drink.' He patted the cushions of a faded yellow sofa against the wall. The telephone rang. Randall Bond picked up the receiver.

'I'm busy, dear,' he said to whoever was calling, but then he went on talking – a conversation about a party and someone named Stella. As he talked, Kate's eyes adjusted to the dim light inside the apartment, and she saw there were stains on the rug and grease spots on the arms of the sofa. There was no maid. Paint was flaking from leaks in the ceiling. A poster of a French château, Azay-le-Rideau, was tacked to the plaster above the bureau, but otherwise there was little sign that anyone lived there except the mess – ashtrays overflowing, clothes on the floor, and a half-empty glass on a table in the entryway. Looking toward the back of the room, Kate saw an overgrown yard through a barred window. The couch she was sitting on must be Randall Bond's bed.

'Let me get you a drink, my dear, a glass of wine,' he said. He had hung up the telephone and turned to her, but suddenly Kate wanted to leave. The effect of Randall Bond's apartment was the same as the effect of all those other weaknesses she had noticed in other men. Before, she had been exhilarated by his interest, because she thought he was the kind of man who could have a beautiful, normal girl if he wanted one, and his interest had made her feel beautiful and normal.

'We'll have a better time if you have some wine with me,' Randall Bond was saying. He brandished a wine bottle in her direction. The glass he poured for himself looked dirty.

'No thank you,' Kate said. How would she get out of here?

'What's the matter, love?'

'Nothing.'

'Are you frightened?' He sat down next to her on the sofa and took her hand. She noticed the cracked leather of his shoes and torn seam inside his tweed jacket. His other arm slid along the sofa above her shoulders.

'No,' she said.

'I find you so lovely, the way you took my hand when we were having coffee, just like a child. I could feel your body against my thigh.'

Yes, it was true. She had touched Randall Bond, she had pressed against him under the greasy Formica table in the coffee shop, but now the thought seemed abhorrent. Randall Bond wasn't a dashing stranger at all. He was a shabby, abject, out-of-work actor, living in a sleazy, dark apartment. He was a loser. He was probably lonelier than she was!

'I could fancy you, sweet,' he was saying now, his head next to hers against the back of the sofa. He spoke close to her ear.

'Has a man ever kissed your breasts, Kate? Has a man ever made love to you and made you come?'

'No,' Kate said. She sat straight up and leaned away from him although his hand was on her shoulder now. She felt sorry for Randall Bond. He seemed pathetic, and the whole idea of sex with him or anyone seemed completely impossible. In fact, a man had never even kissed her lips. The images that he used seemed unlikely and barbaric – a world away from the warm, tingling feelings she had had toward him when their bodies first touched on the bench at the Frick.

'You don't know what you're missing,' he said.

'I don't want to know.'

'You little bitch.' Randall Bond got up off the sofa and walked toward the door. 'Why don't you get the hell out of here, then.'

Kate picked up her guitar and her book of poems and left, opening the door and then the wrought-iron gate and stepping into the sunlight on the sidewalk with relief. The air felt cold as she walked down to Grand Central. It wasn't evening yet, but she might as well go home. Nothing else was going to happen today.

But at night, safe in her own bed upstairs with the school banners and pictures of The Beatles and her books spread out on the desk, Kate remembered the feelings she had had about Randall Bond before they went to his apartment. She remembered the warmth of her body where he brushed against her, and the promises he seemed to be making.

After that, when she was in the city, Kate sometimes wished that she would meet Randall Bond, and that, somehow, things would go differently. She watched for him in museums, or when she walked in the streets near his apartment. Once she thought she saw his handsome head in a crowd of people crossing 72nd Street, but when she ran to catch up, it wasn't him.

· 45 ·

Macklin Riley was now half an hour late. Kate wandered into the Frick Library where Henry Clay Frick's ornate desk sat under the Constable painting of Salisbury Cathedral. The cows were wading in the gentle river, grazing on green meadows with the square tower of the cathedral in the background, just as they had been last year, and on the day she met Randall Bond. Suddenly, Riley was there, walking toward her across the room.

'Hi,' he said, 'I had a little trouble finding you, what was this, some guy's mansion?'

'Henry Clay Frick,' Kate said. Now they had passed into the middle room on the west side of the building, and stood in front of the Bellini portrait of St. Francis. In the painting, the saint stands on a rocky ledge with his hands forward in a gesture both beckoning and imploring. His robes are simple, the colors faded blues and browns. Behind him in a cave are the tools of religious meditation: a table, a book, a human skull. This is the serious St. Francis, a philosopher for the Lord, an accepter of the violence in nature – not the fatuous twittering friend of birds and small animals.

'Who's that?' Riley asked.

'St. Francis, of course, don't you think it's beautiful?'

'A little weird. Anyway, I have my own tastes in painting.'

'You mean those things you have by, what's-her-name, Mina Jonque?' Kate couldn't keep the incredulity out of her voice. How could he compare those to this sublime painting?

'I didn't feel really sure about Mina's paintings at first, but Ann has helped me see that they are good, that my judgment's okay. She and Dorothy have bought some of the paintings, and that's the highest compliment. It's nice to have my taste confirmed by people who know as much as they do. What's the skull? An old enemy?'

'Meditation, thinking about death, maybe you should have one.' She reached out to stroke Riley's arm in a conciliatory gesture. Maybe she had been too mean, but he winced and moved away.

'I'm sorry,' he said, 'I've had a bad day, this place gives me the creeps.'

'But it's one of the finest collections in the city!'

'I'm sure. It's not that – all this furniture, the curtains, the whole thing.' He was silent for a moment. 'I know I shouldn't be so uptight about it,' he said.

'You're a natural aristocrat,' Kate said. 'It doesn't matter what you do or don't have or where you went to school.' They walked past the darkness in the entrance hall and out onto the steps.

'It's a lovely day,' Riley said. Kate could feel his relief at being outdoors, away from the confines of things he didn't understand.

Fifth Avenue comes to a hill in front of the Frick, with one side sloping south toward the towers of midtown, which looks like a city made from children's blocks, and the other side sloping north toward elegant brick and granite apartment houses. These blocks with their liveried doormen, opulent plantings, and gleaming green and brown canopies, are the wealthiest part of the city, and they seem like another metropolis, empty and clean, with a few servants in white uniforms pushing prams or walking sets of tiny dogs into the park. The trees and lawns of Central Park are screened with a low stone wall. The paving is set with octagonal stones, and an allée of sycamores separates the promenade from the street. As they walked, Kate tried to get up the nerve to ask Mack back to her apartment. It would have to be done off-handedly, almost as if it were a joke.

'I have to go back to work,' Riley said, interrupting her

plotting, but he sat down on one of the benches against the wall and smiled up at Kate.

'Sit,' he patted the wooden slats next to him. A squirrel hopped under the bench, picking up acorns. Kate sat as close as she dared.

'I'm sorry you weren't comfortable,' she said. Outside of the hospital or the hospital context, she wondered if he was comfortable anywhere.

'It was my idea, Ann told me about the place, thanks for showing me around.' His arm was draped across the bench behind her. She moved her body close to his.

'Everyone has bad days,' she said.

'Yeah, but so many?'

'This whole situation is so confusing,' Kate said. 'I mean there's you and me and my mother and Ann and her mother,' she shrugged. 'Maybe we should stop.'

'Do you want to stop?' he asked.

'No, but I wish I knew where we were going.'

'Kate, no one knows what's going to happen,' Riley said as he leaned toward her and with infinite gentleness pushed back a lock of her hair and turned to look into her face. 'But you're the important one.'

Buses and cars thumped by on Fifth Avenue. A woman walked by with a small brown mop of a dog on a braided leather leash. The little dog squatted on the ornamental paving stones and emitted a tiny defecation.

'Good girl, oh what a good girl,' the woman crooned. She bent down to pick it up with a page from *Women's Wear Daily*. Summer was over, and Kate shivered in the wind blowing up the avenue from downtown, covering the sidewalk with brown leaves.

· 46 ·

Ann Lacey leaned down over the bed. Her mother's delicate perfume mingled with the smells of sickness, sweat, and the antiseptic aromas of medicine. Visiting her mother in the house was almost as bad as visiting her at the hospital. Now she was at home, but Mack wanted her back for observation. The house seemed empty, the rooms abandoned and musty and the furniture ready for dust covers.

The housekeeper flitted up and down the stairs trying to be invisible. Ann wished she would make more noise. The hushed silence of the house made her sad; there were ghosts already. The ghost of her father, who was always away. She could still see him, bounding up those stairs on his way to her room after a trip, carrying wonderful presents. The ghost of her mother, whose presence had made the place teem and swirl with life. The ghosts of company, of her mother's friends coming by for bridge or tea, of the great parties her mother gave at Christmas, for Ann's wedding, of the glittering guests and the grateful cooks and butlers and maids who had always been glad to work for Mrs. Clay.

'I love you, Mummy,' Ann said in a whisper to her mother's sleeping face. Her features seemed to have grown larger, and had a kind of nobility in repose, a quality neither masculine nor feminine but ageless, as if her character was finally clearly written there. The sheets and pillow cases had a border of braided blue flowers. Ann remembered all the conversations she had had with her mother in this room. She had lain on the chaise over by the window while her mother sat and braided her hair or did her needlepoint. Long afternoons had passed while they tried on each other's clothes or gossiped about the neighbors, or talked about Ann's friends or boyfriends, and about Scott Lacey.

Her mother had understood perfectly why she wanted to marry Scott Lacey, as she understood about them being separated now, and as she understood about Macklin Riley.

Her father had taken a different tack. If my little girl wants it, she will have it – that was his attitude. What he didn't realize was that that left her just as much alone as if he had been indifferent. He never asked why she wanted something. He never took the time to help her distinguish between real need and self-indulgent whim, or between love and desire. Whatever she wanted, he bought for her. If it couldn't be bought, he found a way, through power and connections, to get it. It had taken Ann a long time to see that he wasn't doing this for her – he was doing it for himself.

Ann was used to getting what she wanted. For a while she had wanted Scott Lacey, and they had had a lovely time. He was just who she wanted to be with on the beach at Little Dix, or at the tennis club, or when they went skiing. Because he had such astonishing natural physical grace, because he was so good at everything, Ann had just assumed he would be good at anything.

She had been wrong. When her mother got sick, it became clear what Scott wasn't good at. He wasn't good at feelings. All that grace and ease and physical power didn't translate into compassion or understanding. Sickness frightened and depressed him. He tried to pretend it wasn't happening, and he expected the same behavior from Ann. When she tried to wring sympathy from him, he sulked.

Yes, Ann Lacey was used to getting what she wanted. She was used to getting the clothes she wanted and the business deals she wanted and the men and women she wanted. If it was a question of money or power, her father would take care of it. If it was something more complicated, like making honors at school, or running a business, well that was just a matter of intelligence and hard work, and she knew how to do that. If it was a person, she could be charming, seductive. That was easy. But now, for the first time, she wanted something she couldn't have, and she wanted it more than she had ever wanted anything. She wanted her mother back.

· 47 ·

'Hi, Kate.' It was Macklin Riley's deep, soft voice. 'I'm calling from the corner.'

'Which corner?' Kate had been at her desk, trying to concentrate on the Picasso industry. Mack!

'Across the street, the pay phone on Lexington, maybe you've noticed it in the ten years you've lived here?'

'Do you want to come up?' Kate looked down at her faded denim skirt, her scuffed sandals.

'What a gracious invitation.'

'Just ring the bell.'

As she waited Kate combed out her hair, which had been braided, letting it fall down her back, and kicked off her sandals. Should she meet him with no clothes on? Should she be nude and draped over the daybed? Was he coming to make love to her again? The doorbell rang.

'Hi, come in, what a surprise, how nice,' Kate chattered. She had thought about him coming back here so much that his actual physical presence seemed slightly unreal. Instead of his blazer he wore a faded green polo shirt and jeans, and the green shirt made his face pale and his eyes colorless.

'Want something to drink, coffee? I can heat up some water.' He dismissed her nervous hostessing with a headshake, leaning against the wall and looking around the small room as if it didn't quite match what he remembered. Kate willed him to sink down on the daybed and open his arms to her the way he had before, the way men do in romantic novels.

'Don't you understand,' he would say. 'It was you I loved all along, you little fool.'

Instead he stared out the dirty windows at the overcast autumn sky.

'It's Wednesday, don't you have afternoon clinic today?'

'I switched with Kellner, I just couldn't face it.'

'Anything in particular?'

'Nothing really, just my inability to detach, it gets to me after a while.'

'Of course it does.'

'There are so many times when there's nothing I can do. Even when medicine can succeed, half the time people don't take advantage of it, look at you with your leg for instance.

'We've gone over this before, I'm thinking about it. It's not that I reject what medicine can do, it's that I'm used to it the way it is.' Why were they talking about her leg when they should be talking about love?

'You could have the whole thing reset, it would be normal, wouldn't that be a relief?' Riley seemed to have cheered up now, he stood up straight and spoke with enthusiasm.

'It's my leg, it's more than just a medical anachronism,' she said, 'maybe I've gotten used to it.'

'It's not going to get better, you know. If you wanted to have a child, any added stress, it might get worse.' Riley was maddeningly uninvolved when he talked about her. He didn't include himself in her future – certainly not as the father of her child.

'I don't care,' Kate said. Now Riley sighed and sat down heavily on the daybed, extending his long legs.

'That's stupid, of course you care,' he said.

'Let's not fight,' Kate said, 'you're tired.' She knelt at his feet and slipped off his brown tasseled loafers. Slowly she began massaging his feet and lower legs. 'You need a break,' she said.

Riley inhaled and exhaled loudly. 'That feels nice,' he said. Kate stroked his legs and he closed his eyes.

'I can feel you relaxing,' she said. Now she gently spread his thighs and perched between them on the daybed, raising her hands to grasp and massage his neck and shoulders.

'Mmmmm,' Riley said. His eyes were still closed as she leaned forward to kiss him. She could feel her nerves loosening, her body responding to his closeness. His rough skin smelled faintly of alcohol and cloves. Putting her hands behind his head, Kate planted little kisses on his neck and around his ears.

'I've missed you,' she said.

'Katie,' he said, 'we can't.' He rubbed her back with the flat of his hand. The gesture was affectionate and not sexual.

'Why not?'

'It's not that I'm not turned on, you're very attractive, you know that, it's the hospital, a lot of reasons. You're married, for God's sake.'

'But we did, it was wonderful, it was so nice.' Kate leaned her body into his. 'Remember?'

'It was nice.'

'Who would know?'

'We'd know.' Now Riley gently pushed against her and stood up. 'Maybe I just can't explain it right now. I shouldn't have come up here.'

'Maybe you came because you wanted . . .'

'All the more reason why I shouldn't have.'

Kate stood next to him. He was trying not to reject her, but he was rejecting her. Pain seemed to seep through her skin from his direction. She wouldn't let him see it. He walked to the door, and she opened it for him with a smile.

'Have it your way,' she said. As they waited for the elevator, he put a hand on her shoulder and let it drift up to her chin. The elevator was coming. He was safe now.

'You're a funny girl,' he said.

'We're both pretty stubborn.' He stepped into the elevator and the door slammed shut. The visit was over.

Kate shut her own door and stood staring out of the window. Her senses had been altered by the sexual contact with Riley's body so that she felt displaced, as if she were the same person in a different body. She was glad that she had matched his cool, but that didn't make her feel cool. How could she get through the rest of the afternoon? The rest of the day? The rest of her life? The sky outside cleared leaving wisps of blue above the other apartment buildings. Kate began to relax.

Later that afternoon, as she was typing some notes from a telephone conversation, her typewriter stopped suddenly in the middle of a word. She pressed the code buttons and the On and Off button, but the machine was dead. Behind the desk, she switched on a lamp – nothing happened. The electricity was off. None of the lights worked. The clock had stopped at 2:46 P.M.

Kate went out into the hall and around the corner toward Madame Barthélemy's room and stood under the fuse box, but it was too high for her to reach. She went back into her office, picked up one of the chairs that she had salvaged from her parents' attic, and dragged it down the hall. Madame Barthélemy's door was closed, and there was no sign of her except a slight dampness where the hall had been recently mopped. Standing on the chair, Kate opened the gray, metal fuse box and studied the three rows of glass fuses with their yellow tabs. None of them looked blown, but by twisting each one, she found that the first three in the middle row – the ones that controlled the current for her office – had been loosened until the connection was broken. She tightened them and closed the box, picked up her chair and took it back to her desk. The lights worked again. The typewriter hummed. She had to reset the clock.

· 48 ·

Kate drove out along the Saw Mill to visit her mother. The leaves had turned red and gold, and there was the smell of apples and burning leaves in the air, although these days it was against the law to burn leaves – you were supposed to stuff them into plastic bags and let the garbagemen take them away. As she slowed to drive through town, past the fake-Tudor shop fronts and gas stations that she had known for so long, she saw school children on their way home, loaded down with books.

It had been six weeks since the end of the radiation treatments, and five months since the day when her mother was diagnosed as having cancer. It seemed a lot longer. At the end of the treatments, her mother had looked frighteningly sick. Her skin was waxy, and she lost weight. Now that she was better, she looked the way she had a year ago. All there was to do was wait, and go back in six months for a checkup. Either the cancer would come back, perhaps in some other part of the body where it might be impossible to treat, or the cancer wouldn't come back at all.

Kate's mother came out to greet her with a kiss. She was cheerful, but when they went indoors Kate saw that the kitchen was still in terrible disarray. There were dishes piled in the sink. The cookie jar was empty and a broken cracker moldered at the bottom of it. In the refrigerator was a half-eaten container of yogurt, an old head of lettuce still in a plastic bag, and a piece of cheese with green mold growing in streaks on one side.

'Are you feeling all right? Everything okay?' Kate asked.

They stood together in the kitchen waiting for the water to boil for tea. When Kate opened the cupboard to look for tea bags, an empty bag of cookies and an open can of coffee fell out onto the counter; she caught the coffee before it spilled and pushed the plastic top down firmly over the edge of the can before putting it back. Deeper in, behind some old cereal boxes, she found a crushed box of tea bags.

'Oh, I'm fine,' her mother said. 'I wish everyone would stop acting as if I were so sick. You know who's been coming over a lot lately?'

'Un unh,' Kate had extracted a bag from the crushed box and dropped it into one of the cups on the dish-draining rack.

'Don, you know Don Anderson, he comes by almost every day now.'

'That's nice.' Don Anderson was a burly blond computer analyst who lived across the street from the Loomis property. He always had a tan, and Kate had sometimes wondered if his hair was bleached. His wife had left him a few years ago, and he had stayed in the boxy modern house they had built together. Kate didn't think she had ever heard Don Anderson actually speak. Before she left, his wife had always spoken for him, 'We think this, and we think that,' she would say. Recently he seemed to have lapsed into permanent taciturnity. Usually he just stood around and flexed his muscles, developed in workouts at the local gym. Kate vaguely remembered hearing that Don Anderson was a vegetarian and that he had taken up yoga. She hadn't listened very carefully.

'He thinks I'm wonderful.' Her mother giggled.

'That's nice, Mom,' Kate said, she poured the boiling water into her cup.

'He started me doing yoga for my back, and it's the one thing that's really helped. All those doctors! He says I shouldn't trust doctors, they don't know anything about nutrition or health – they only know about disease.'

'Whatever happened to his wife?'

'She's off in Hawaii somewhere; they're divorced now

anyway. I tell him I'm too old for him.' Her mother giggled again.

'Who cares how old you are?' Kate said, but the thought of Don Anderson, the computer whiz and ex-surfer, moving in on her mother, disturbed her. Did he want her money? It was all protected in trust. He was lonely; she was lonely.

'Have some honey,' her mother said. 'I don't think I have any sugar, Don says it's bad for me anyway.'

Kate looked. The sugar bowl was empty except for two round lumps hardening at the bottom. She plunged a spoon into the honey jar and then into her steaming cup of tea. Although it was still early afternoon, the kitchen was dark. The big porch on the front of the house cut out the light.

'There's nothing quite as comforting as a cup of tea on a cool afternoon,' her mother said. 'Don't you love that honey? It's a jar that Deirdre brought me from Vermont.' Matilda's friend Deirdre had moved back from Vermont two years before. Her mother sipped her own cup of tea. 'I'm so glad you don't mind the ants,' her mother said. 'Don says the formic acid is probably good for us.'

Looking more carefully, Kate saw that tiny, black ants were pooled at the bottom of the honey jar, and that the spoon she had used to serve the honey had twirled a stream of ants into her cup of tea. She put the cup down on the counter.

'Is he getting really serious about you? I mean, remember how we used to laugh at him, Mom?'

'That was your father's sarcasm,' her mother said. 'I always thought he was a very decent man, very good-hearted.'

'I'm sure he's good-hearted, but, Mom, those biceps!'

'How a person looks doesn't really matter to me, I guess,' her mother said.

'He may be nice, he may be good-hearted, but he's certainly not the perfect man,' Kate said. She was irritated by the idea of Don Anderson taking her father's place and irritated by the ants in the tea.

'Is David so perfect? You don't always make him sound that way.'

'David? Why, you can't even compare them.' Kate had been about to point out that David was her age at least, that she and David had the same background, that David was appropriate. She stopped. Weren't those also the things that were wrong with David?

'I *can* compare them, I think David's very cold sometimes, you two act as if you have a marriage of convenience. Don and I are friends, we have warm feelings about each other.'

'David's not so bad.' Her mother's attack made Kate feel defensive and protective of David and of their marriage.

'He doesn't understand you very well sometimes.'

Kate thought about David in his office, David taking her out to lunch and being supportive of her in her quarrels with editors.

'He understands me pretty well,' she said.

· 49 ·

'They've decided not to do another operation, Dorothy,' Macklin Riley said. He picked a black and gold pen off the Formica surface of his desk. Ann sat opposite him on the little couch, and her mother sat in a chair with her back to the overflowing bookshelves.

'Why not?' Dorothy Clay asked. It was still early in the morning. A half-eaten corn muffin lay crumbled on a paper plate next to Dr. Riley's telephones.

'Your white-blood-cell count, there are a lot of things. They've decided it wouldn't be a good idea right now.'

'They? I thought you were my doctor.'

'The surgeons, in this case Fred Bingham, make the final decisions about surgery, and I agree.'

'So will there be more chemotherapy, do the tests affect that?'

'Right now, the best thing seems to be to suspend treatment. We've finished the course from Tehualtepec Clinic, and in fact I'm going to send you home today. That should be good news.' Riley capped and uncapped the black and gold pen.

'It didn't really work, did it, the Mexican stuff?' Dorothy Clay sat upright, concentrating all her remaining shreds of energy on the conversation. Her short hair, just beginning to grow back after the chemotherapy treatment, emphasized her sharp, hawklike nose and blue eyes. A lot of women at the hospital hid their heads under turbans or special little flowered triangles that were for sale downstairs in the gift shop. Dorothy Clay did not hide.

'No,' he said. He looked down at the desk.

'Mack,' Dorothy Clay's voice was even and steady. 'Mack, are you sending me home to die?' Ann was surprised by the blunt question, but she kept quiet. This was between her mother and Mack, but she noticed that in spite of her steady voice, her mother's eyes were shining. Above Mack on his office shelf, where a different kind of man might have hung a crucifix, or a picture of a mentor or parent, Ann noticed a blue and orange baseball cap. Mack had told her about Eddie Gomez, the little boy who died.

'I didn't say that, Dorothy, I didn't say anything *like* that. It's just that at the moment, further treatment doesn't seem like a good idea. I thought you might be pleased.'

'I need to know, Mack. There are business decisions to be made, the insurance companies have to be dealt with. There are trusts too, most of them in my name, and if Ann were to remarry that has to be provided for, please.' Ann sat and listened. This was a situation her mother could handle better than she could, even now. In her own conversations with Mack, she had been unable to get a time limit out of him, or even get him to speculate on how long her mother might live. Anyone could see it wasn't long. Somehow Mack's opinion, his confirmation of her fears, was important to her. Instead, he always wanted to talk about medicine, or about his own plans, or hers.

'Dorothy,' he was saying now, 'if I knew, I would tell you. I don't usually do that, but I would tell you. It's true that the operations haven't been as successful as we had hoped, and we're still not sure about the effects of the various drugs you've had administered. We have no real evidence that the disease has spread farther than the abdomen, none at all.' Riley leaned forward across his desk, as if he could persuade this woman by getting closer to her. He capped and uncapped the black and gold pen. His fingers were white from gripping the narrow cylinder.

'I'm not asking for anything impossible, Mack, I know that no one can be certain about these things, I just need to know what you know. We've become friends, and our friendship and your friendship with Ann have meant a great deal to me. I like to think there will be someone . . .' Dorothy Clay bowed her head for a moment. An office cart rattled by in the hallway, in the distance Ann could hear a murmured conversation. Her mother looked up again; she had recovered her force. 'Do you think it's months or weeks? There's a big difference for the business if I make it through January first. It's October now, can you at least give me an estimate?'

'We can never be sure of these things,' Riley's tone was patient now, as if he was reasoning with a child. 'You look very well today, Dorothy, but based on other patients I have seen in similar situations, I just think it's time for you to go home – you do better there anyway. That's all I can tell you.'

'But based on other patients you have seen with systemic disease, other patients with breast cancer metastasized to the abdomen?' Ann saw that the effort was tiring her mother. She had gathered all her energy for this encounter, and it was fading. It was so easy for Mack to outlast her! Ann had a flash of rage at him, in spite of everything he had done, in spite of her other feelings. It wasn't fair. Her mother's face looked thinner now, even thinner, and the bones seemed to push at the flesh as if there were pressure from inside. She was sagging in the chair, and Ann leaned forward so that she could catch her mother if she fell.

'It's impossible to tell, really,' Mack was saying, 'and based on some of my other patients, you are actually doing very well.' Some of his other patients are dead, Ann thought, but she stayed silent. She knew that her anger at Mack was sympathy for her mother, her mother who, even now, insisted on using the word death and avoided the ridiculous hospital euphemisms, passing on, leaving this world.

'Mack, if I'm going to die before the first of the year, it's very important for me to reinsure some departments in the company and some aspects of the estate. It's expensive, I wouldn't usually do it now. Do you think I should do that?' Dorothy Clay had drawn herself up straight in her chair again. Now Ann slumped on the sofa.

'Yes, I think you should,' Macklin Riley said. The black and gold cap bent under the pressure of his fingers.

'Thank you, Mack,' Dorothy's voice faded quickly to a whisper. Her strength was gone, Ann quickly took her arm as she tried to rise from the chair, and Mack took her other arm.

'Let me get a wheelchair,' he said. In the minute he was gone, Ann watched her mother's eyes close with exhaustion.

'Just get me home,' she said. Mack was back with the wheelchair, and Dorothy fell asleep as they wheeled her out through the halls to the parked car. When they got there, Mack lifted her out of the chair as if she were a child and tenderly laid her sleeping body on the back seat, covering her with a light blanket. Then he walked around to where Ann sat at the wheel.

'Are you okay?' He laid his hand against the side of her face.

'I'm not sure,' she said, leaning down to take off the brake.

'I wish I could come with you,' he said.

'But you have other patients.'

'Call me when you get home,' he said, and he watched as she drove down East End and turned right at 79th Street.

Back in his office, Riley put the chair Dorothy had been sitting in against the wall. It was still early, the telephone didn't ring. For a while he sat on the desk with his head in his hands. Then he took the windup animals down from the shelf, avoiding the baseball cap with his eyes. Carefully he wound them, the bear with the drum, the monkeys with cymbals, and the cat playing the violin, holding their stems so that when he let them go they all played together. It didn't help. He was still seeing Ann and her mother, two noble women, still watching Ann drive off down East End Avenue, still wondering if Dorothy would sleep all the way home to Greenwich. He got up and paced back and forth, longing for distractions, the telephone, his beeper.

This wasn't the first time he had had to tell a patient she was going to die, but it was the first time he realized what it meant. Maybe Eddie Gomez's death had shaken him. Riley remembered Kate Weiss complaining that, for the patient and the family, those conferences in the examining rooms were the worst, most frightening moments of their lives – whereas for the doctor they were just another incident in just another day. Each death in the hospital shattered a family and lives outside the hospital. But for the doctors a single death was nothing unusual, the termination of another case. No matter how he tried, Riley couldn't think of Dorothy Clay as just another patient or this morning as just another day, or of Ann as just another attractive woman.

He dialed the Clay number in Greenwich, but no one answered. They must still be on the road, but it had been more than an hour. He began to worry. He called Ann's office, but her secretary said she wasn't expected. He called Ann's house and got the answering service, but he hung up instead of leaving a message. Then he called Kate.

· 50 ·

'It's Mack,' he said.

'Hi,' she tried to keep her voice from squeaking into the upper registers. Her throat felt dry.

'Is this a bad moment?'

'Oh, no, just working.' As if there were anything in the world she wouldn't drop if he called. 'How's it going over there?'

'Okay. How's your mother doing?'

'She's all right, she's got a new boyfriend, she seems to have recovered from the treatments. Have I thanked you enough for everything you did for her?'

'That's my job.'

'You did much more than your job.'

'Listen, would you like to have lunch or something? I'm at the office now, but I have to go down to the new apartment. Drop by, and I'll fix us something.'

'Can I bring anything?' Kate asked.

'Just your good cheer,' Riley said.

It was one of those autumn days in New York when the sky is so clear that downtown looks like a postcard, and people are out in their new tweeds and leathers and gabardine clothes. The trees were still red and gold and Lexington was crowded with shoppers. There were Halloween pumpkins and masks in the windows of florist shops, and a display of Pilgrims and turkeys in the window of a toy store on 69th Street.

The Ascot had a deserted look. There was one doorman at the revolving glass and brass door, and one elevator man in front of the marble floor panels. Kate felt buoyantly alone and anonymous being swept up through this shining glass plinth to a romantic tryst.

The halls upstairs were silent and empty, and Riley's door was wide open, as if he were the only occupant of the floor. He was sitting on a chair staring down the side street toward the river. Looking around him, Kate saw that although Riley had moved weeks ago, not very much had been unpacked. There were piles of boxes stacked against the walls and torn, heavy brown paper, cardboard, and twine on the floor where some packages had been opened. Except for that one rainy afternoon, she had rarely seen Riley without other people, and without the paraphernalia of his office, or the ringing and beeping sounds that went with his job. Now, with no one competing for his attention, he looked lonely and a little forlorn. When she stepped off the carpet in the foyer and into the living room, her footsteps echoed on the floor, and he jumped up and smiled.

'Hi, it's great to see you!'

Kate smiled back.

'I've been thinking too much,' Riley said. 'I'm really glad you came by.'

'I don't think I've ever seen you sit still before,' she said. 'It's not as if there isn't a lot to do right here.' With a nod she indicated the unpacked boxes, the mess of twine and paper on the floor.

'Oh, God, you know how it is, I haven't even had time to unpack. I shouldn't even be here, I just came home because it was a bad morning, probably a mistake.'

'A mistake in my favor,' Kate said, 'since it means I get to have lunch with you.' She was consciously aware of flattering him. Riley seemed slightly off balance without his props, without his patients waiting for him and his piles of message slips and his rude secretaries. Kate noticed that his thick, dark hair was oily at the sides, and he had cut himself shaving, leaving a small row of scabs on his jaw.

'Let's have a glass of wine,' he said, 'come on, sit down.' He pointed to the other chair – two chairs were the only furniture that had been unpacked besides a long, slate coffee table. As she sat, Kate heard the noises of a bottle of wine being opened in the kitchen around the corner. First, Macklin Riley's grunt as he drove in the corkscrew, then the low squeal of cork against glass as he turned it, and finally the pop as the cork came out of the bottle. There were no other noises to shatter the stillness. If people lived in The Ascot they must be away. Kate remembered Riley's old apartment and how it had been teeming, reverberating with life, the noises of the neighbors' television sets, the smells of cooking, the cockroach.

Far below her, through the window at the edge of the room, she could see crowds pouring out of their office buildings at lunchtime, women in tweed suits and men with briefcases or with overcoats thrown over their arms because it was turning warm; honking traffic was building up at the entrance to the bridge. Indian summer. Indoors, everything was automatically temperate. The tinted double-paned windows made the world outside seem foreign and distant, as if she and Dr. Riley were traveling through mobbed, hot streets in an air-cooled limousine behind drawn shades.

On the way back from the kitchen, Mack set the bottle of wine and two glasses down on the coffee table and went over to the tape deck that sat on the floor next to a packing box. In a moment, the melancholy strings of Violetta's overture filled the room, sharpening Kate's sense of the romantic interlude and reinforcing the impression that she and Mack were in a world all their own.

'This is a treat,' he said, handing her a glass. He sat down next to her on a packing box. 'I've been brooding.'

'I thought doctors didn't have time to brood.'

'They're not supposed to, but it was another bad day. I had to tell someone something she didn't want to hear.'

'Let me guess.'

'You know what it was, the surprising thing was how it felt.'

'You can't blame yourself when that happens. It's not your fault, Mack.'

'I know that, but it doesn't always help.'

'It doesn't happen because of you, it happens in spite of you. Because of what you do, a lot of people live.'

'Still it always feels like a failure, a rebuke to my skill. I know so much, I should have been able to do something.'

'You're bound to feel that way because you're compassionate, which is rare enough – just don't go thinking it's your responsibility. That's arrogant!'

'I know you're right.'

'You just can't believe it.'

'Right again.' Riley stared at the floor and the cardboard of the packing case sagged under his weight. Kate sipped her wine, it was slightly sweet. His glass was empty, and he reached forward to pour himself another and add to hers.

'You know a lot,' he said, 'for a woman as attractive as you are.'

'Everyone in the world knows you can't take responsibility for what happens to other people,' she said. She liked 'attractive' but she wondered if he was trying to change the subject. It was easier for him to talk about other people's problems.

'Maybe it's your leg,' he said. 'What happened. . . . Have you thought about what I said?'

'I've thought about it.' She was right.

'Not that it's so noticeable.'

'Besides, it makes me different from other women, don't you think? I'm not just another of your bimbos. I've met adversity and overcome it, blah blah blah, it makes me more interesting, don't you think?'

'You are *very* interesting. I think you'd be just as interesting with a fully functional knee.'

Kate stood up and stepped over the stack of flattened cardboard boxes and twine toward the windows. She had finished the wine in her refilled glass, and her head felt light. Everything seemed to have lost its sharp edges; her thinking blurred. Mack Riley had loved her, slept with her, announced that he couldn't sleep with her anymore, and now seemed to be inviting her to sleep with him again. She was tired of confusion. Maybe she was crazy, and he was right, maybe hospitals were good for people, maybe she was being stubborn.

Outside the colors of the late autumn day seemed to have intensified. Kate thought that she was in love with Macklin Riley, who was sititng a few feet behind her, but she wished that she was out of there, down there far below on the street, free of him. Looking down, she saw the tiny figures of men and women like the drawn figures in an architect's plan, and she envied them their simple, busy lives, their having somewhere to go in such a hurry.

When Kate wasn't with him, she knew that Riley was the perfect man, the understanding and compassionate one she had always known she would meet someday. All her life she had been straining toward a someone, and she often felt that, if she were with Riley, the rest of her life would fall magically into place.

But now he was depressed. He seemed kind of pathetic, the way he needed her reassurance. She turned away from the window and faced him.

'I think I should go,' she said, 'this has been nice.' Riley put his wineglass down on the floor and looked up at her.

'Come here,' he said.

Kate had wanted Mack to make love to her again so intensely, that when he finally did it seemed to be happening to someone else. His kisses, which in her memory had sent her into a swoon, felt rough, and his breath smelled slightly of wine. There was nowhere to lie down in his apartment, so he laid her down on a bed of cardboard and pushed up her sweater and pulled down her pants. He didn't take off his shirt this time. The edge of the cardboard carton where she lay gouged into her back, and a piece of twine rubbing against her thigh as he pushed himself into her felt as if it were cutting into her flesh. Even with Riley on top of her, her mind wandered, wondering how she would explain the sore to David.

That didn't matter, she reminded herself. This was what

she wanted, Mack's loving. But what if he acted the same way this time? What if he pretended this hadn't happened, that it meant nothing, that they were just friends. She tried to push the thought away. In the background, Alfredo's father pleaded with his son to forsake Violetta and return home to beautiful Provence.

Afterward they leaned together against one of the chairs. Kate rubbed the back of her thigh. The skin was sore, but smooth and unscarred.

'Did I hurt you?' he asked.

'No,' she kissed his shoulder.

'Sex is so great,' he said.

'With you it is.'

'You are wonderful.'

'And you.' Riley kissed her on the cheek and spread his naked legs out on the wooden floor.

'I feel a lot better,' he said. A sharp pinging sound came from behind the chair – his beeper.

'Oh Christ!' he said, but it seemed to be a summons he was somehow waiting for. He rolled over and stood up, keeping his back to her as he pulled on his pants and disappeared into the other room. As she put her clothes back in order, Kate could hear his deep authoritative doctor's voice on the telephone.

'Don't start treatment yet,' he was saying. 'I'd like to see if she's estrogen receptor positive.' Then there was a silence as he listened. 'I'll meet you in my office before clinic this afternoon,' he said, 'about one, are there any messages?'

Kate looked at the watch her father had given her when she graduated from college. It was ten minutes to one. Mack Riley appeared in the doorway buckling his belt.

'I have to go back to the hospital, Babe,' he said.

'Okay.' Kate finished dressing and slipped on her shoes. Soon it would be cold enough to wear boots. Together they left the apartment, Riley turned the key in the lock, and they walked down the silent carpeted hallway toward the elevators. As they waited for the car, Kate touched Riley's arm to get his attention.

'So now that you've had your way with me, I guess I won't be hearing from you again.' She giggled to show that this was a joke. After all, this wasn't the first time. It was a joke about other men's behavior, a joke that was meant to let him off the hook.

Riley didn't laugh, and when she looked up at him, she saw that, instead of laughing, he had reared back and away from her like a spooked horse, and that there was fear and confusion in his eyes.

'Hey,' she said, 'just a joke.' He didn't answer but kissed her lightly as they parted in the street in front of The Ascot.

· 51 ·

'You're home early,' Kate said. She headed for the shower, irritated at David for being there when she hadn't counted on that, guilty about sleeping with Riley. 'What's up?'

'Crappy day at work, I just thought I'd take an afternoon off, walk home, maybe read,' David stood in the kitchen and spoke to her through the doorway. 'I'm making some coffee, want some?'

'Sure, let me shower first, I feel grubby.' How could David look at her and not see how changed she was? Kate stayed in the living room, away from him. If he came any closer, she was sure he could smell strange sex on her body, sense the confusion she felt. She was angry at David because she had to lie to him. In the bedroom, she stripped off her clothes and threw them in the laundry hamper, her sweater that Macklin Riley had pulled off her breasts, her pants. Standing under the stream of hot water in the shower, she soaped herself until there was a layer of foam on every inch of her body and then let the water sluice it away. Although she usually washed her hair in the morning, she put her head under the shower now and massaged shampoo into the thick, wet clumps, and then rinsed it out. She would wash the morning away, the smells, the headache from the wine, the look on Riley's face when she had said she wouldn't be hearing from him again.

After her shower she put on a clean shirt and fresh, pressed blue jeans and combed the snarls out of her wet hair. She smelled of soap and starch. David was still in the kitchen.

'What happened at work, anything in particular? It's not like you to come home early.' David was sipping his coffee, the pungent smell of the freshly ground beans filled the kitchen, he held out a cup toward her.

'Do you want some milk?' he asked.

'No thanks, the office?'

'Nothing much.'

'David, if you never talk about your feelings, you'll never understand them. Did something get to you? Is it something I should know about?'

David shrugged. He was still in a business suit and tie, and standing in the kitchen in the middle of the afternoon, he seemed oddly imposing, as if he were still wearing the power of his job.

'I'm not kidding,' Kate said. She sipped her coffee, relishing the rich taste of it and the jolt of energy.

'Do you think you talk about your feelings? Do you think you've been so open with me?' he said.

'That's not the point, you're just defending yourself.'

'I just wondered.'

'Maybe I'm not so open,' Kate said. 'I have the feeling you don't want to hear about my feelings, they're too embarrassing for you, too intense, too inconvenient, they might distract you from your books or some deal.'

David leaned back against the counter and sipped his coffee. His tanned, handsome face looked relaxed, maddeningly unaffected by her tirade.

'That's not fair, Kate.'

'Do you think you're fair to me?'

'I try to be.'

'Do you think it's fair to just sit there like a stone in a ballet while I'm crying? Do you think it's fair to pretend you don't notice when I'm upset?'

'You're pretty angry,' he said. He reached over and poured more coffee into his cup.

'I have a lot to be angry about. You're so unfeeling, you're so unsympathetic. I know we're married, but most of the time I feel completely alone, it's as if we're living together, but we're invisible to each other or something. We don't connect!

Don't you even notice? Don't you even have a little curiosity about how I'm feeling, what's going on with me?' Kate walked out of the kitchen into the living room and stared out at the street. It was still the same afternoon. She cradled her warm coffee cup in her hands.

'Kate, I do care how you're feeling,' David had followed her. Kate collapsed onto the sofa. Venting her anger against David made her feel better, but now confusion raged in her mind. Before, she had used the image of Macklin Riley to answer all her questions. Somehow, she had believed he would make everything clear. Now the questions came tumbling back. What should she do about her marriage? her leg? having a child?

'Oh, I don't know, I'm just confused,' she said. 'Sometimes I get so tired of my life.'

'Let's go away,' David said. 'Remember we used to talk about subletting the apartment, living in France or England for a while? Maybe this is the time. I could give up a year at the firm now, I'm not sure lawyering is what I want to do for the rest of my life anyway.' David walked around the back of the sofa and massaged her shoulders. His hands felt strong, she could feel them pulling the bones together and loosening the nerves under her taut skin.

'Maybe I'm just having an early mid-life crisis,' she said.

'It's not a mystery. You've been under a lot of stress – your father, now your mother sick – and you're getting older.'

'What difference does that make?'

David shrugged. 'It might make a difference.'

'I thought we had decided not to have children,' she said.

'That was a long time ago. We can change our minds, we can do what we want.' Now David came around and sat beside her.

'I don't know what I want, that's the trouble. Whenever I think about it, I get stuck, or I veer in one direction and then the other. It seems to me it would be a disaster if I had a child . . . and a disaster if I didn't.'

'Not really. Other people seem to handle it, I think we probably could.'

'What about my knee?'

'What about it?'

'Some doctor mentioned to me that, if I had a child, it might be too much pressure. He suggested I have it redone, apparently there are new operations now.'

'Well, then?'

'I don't want to do it, my knee is fine, I've gotten used to it.'

'It is fine,' David said. 'God, remember what you went through, no wonder you don't want to have it redone. So, that might make having a child a little harder, it wouldn't make it impossible.'

'It feels overwhelming.'

'I know, I just wanted to say that if you were thinking about it, I'd like to think about it.'

'I'm thinking.'

'It's not something to worry about, whatever has to be done we could have done. Nothing's that difficult.'

Kate leaned against David's shoulder. They had known each other for so long. He had known her as a child; he had known her father. It was nice to have a partner, someone to share things with, someone who automatically shared everything.

'We've been married a long time,' she said.

'I know, sometimes it seems like weeks, and sometimes . . .'

'It seems longer, like aeons?' she laughed.

'You know I was never sure about marrying you, it seemed so automatic,' David said. 'And there were other girls, all the girls in the world I would never be able to marry if I married you. Still, I'm glad I did now.'

'I never thought you hestitated for a minute,' Kate said. She had thought of David as an automaton, a robot, programmed by his parents.

'Well, I didn't exactly think you'd welcome hearing about my doubts,' David laughed. 'Anyway I've grown out of them. You're a wonderful girl,' he said.

'You never say that.'

'I thought you knew.' Late afternoon sun slanted through

the windows and onto the sofa and the heavy Weiss family furniture, the silks and oils and gleaming inlays. Out the window she could see some high clouds in a blue sky and the granite top of the brick apartment across the way.

· 52 ·

It was Halloween at the hospital, and in the halls, a procession of costumed children, some on crutches, some in wheelchairs, visited the patients' rooms and doctors' offices. Trick or treat, they said, trick or treat. Some had been working all day on camouflaging bandages with rabbit or tiger masks, or covering bald heads with elaborate wigs and hats. There was a clown with a white painted face and a red satin ruff collar – a clown in iron braces, and a pirate with a long mustache and an eye patch who flew the Jolly Roger from the top of his IV pole. Volunteers wheeled the chattering group from floor to floor as if this were just any crowd of children dressed up for Halloween. One child, in beggar's rags which covered an abdominal bandage, shook a tin cup. Everyone smiled as they passed. A huge pumpkin with jack-o'-lantern face adorned the main table in the lobby where families waited. There were autumn leaves and cattails in the big vases outside the gift shop.

Dr. Peter Mallory was sitting at the back of the weekly Mortality and Morbidity conference in a small, darkened auditorium off the lobby. Mortality and Morbidity was the conference during which each death among the department's patients was examined and reassessed. Had the doctors gone too far? Had they not gone far enough? The chief of the department described each case, and the doctors who had worked on it explained themselves. Mallory called it quality control. It was hard, in the cool atmosphere of the conference, to re-create the panic and uncertainty of an emergency code, or of the operating room at 2 A.M. No one came to Mortality and Morbidity unless they had to.

Most of the cases were routine. One nineteen-year-old boy with advanced renal cancer had died during a major operation performed by Dr. Kramer. Kramer tried to explain why he had undertaken the operation, when the boy would have died soon anyway. His voice faltered. Surgeons love to operate; they get paid for operating.

Often there had been no mistakes. In cancer treatment everything can be done perfectly from a medical point of view, and still the patient dies. Mallory's case was an eighty-year-old woman on whom he had done an abdominal exploration. The anesthetic and the operation had been too much for her heart. Mallory explained why he had done the exploratory operation – if there had been an isolated tumor, he might have been able to make her much more comfortable with a simple operation, the way he had done with Dan Connors. For a moment, in the dark room, he thought of the old woman draped and under the OR lights, her labored breathing and the anesthesiologist's panicky noises, and then the absence of breathing. Her children and grandchildren had come to visit her before the operation.

In evening clinic, the first patient's folder was marked VIP in discreet red letters. Mallory recognized him of course, the most famous movie star of the eighties; and Mallory's secretary had protected him by whisking him into an examining room and making arrangements for him to leave by the back door. Mallory disapproved of special treatment. He had worked on movie stars and famous writers and heads of state, and the ones he liked the best were the ones who came to clinic and waited along with everyone else.

Usually the VIPs were businessmen, men who had given a lot of money to the hospital – what a difference that made, whether you were a doctor or a patient! Or men who said they were afraid that the news they had cancer might affect the stock market or important company mergers. Mallory didn't think much of that either. Sometimes these big shots came up to his office for their appointments, so that they wouldn't have to wait in clinic with the other patients. Usually they treated him like a personal servant. What they didn't realize was that they got better treatment if they waited along with everyone else. In his office, Mallory had to do his own blood tests, for instance, and he wasn't as good at it as the nurses who did it every day. Private patients set themselves outside the system at their peril – the system worked.

The movie star had a benign lesion on his lower back. Some jerk from the studio where he worked had tried to remove it, and failed. After doing a sloppy operation, he had decided it was cancer. Ignorant panic followed. Mallory was so disgusted that he could barely manage a smile when he told the movie star the good news.

Later, on his way upstairs as he burst out of the fourth floor stairwell, Mallory ran into Mack Riley kissing some girl goodbye, as he ushered her into the elevator. He recognized the girl as the daughter of a patient, the daughter of a patient who had just made a significant gift to the hospital. Although he passed the couple with a friendly nod, Mallory seethed as he walked down to the nurses' station. Macklin Riley's annual evaluation had shown his research to be inadequate and badly prepared. Broders, the head of the hospital, had already suggested to Mallory, more than suggested, that unless there was a dramatic change in his behavior or his circumstances, Riley would have to go. It was Mallory who would have to fire him. And now, instead of being chastened by the evaluation report, and working night and day in the labs, or up in the deparment of biostatistics, here he was carrying on with a nice-looking girl – a patient's daughter.

Mallory had decided at the beginning of his tenure at Parkinson Center not to get involved with patients or their families. He had never broken that rule. He knew that he had kept it out of fear, rather than some abstract virtue. A lot of patients fall in love with their doctors. He was afraid of what could happen if he cared too much about the human dramas in which he was such an unnaturally powerful agent.

What was worse, he liked Riley. The guy was smart, charming, great with patients. Mallory could understand how a doctor might easily, very easily, get involved, too involved to do his best work on other cases, too involved to do his reasearch. He could understand it very well, and that was why he couldn't tolerate it.

· 53 ·

Late in the afternoon, her mother started asking her to call Mack.

'Why?' Ann said, but she did it. Her mother didn't answer. Every word was an effort now, her bones pushed sharply through her papery skin, and she didn't seem to know quite where she was. When Ann asked her questions, she might talk about the past, or talk to Ann as if she were Anita, her own mother on a visit to Turk Cay. Once, at about noontime, she had asked Ann to close the blinds, and Ann could see she thought she was talking to one of the houseboys in the old house on the island. Sometimes she giggled like a girl, or talked to Loki, the retriever they had had when Ann was a child.

Mack arrived as night fell, she heard his tires on the gravel drive. He went right upstairs and didn't come down for two hours. Ann got him a drink.

'Did she talk to you?' she asked.

He laughed. 'I couldn't shut her up, but when she had finished, when she had said everything she had to say, she seemed all right.'

'What did she have to say?'

'She wanted to talk about the past, I guess you heard some of that this afternoon, her sadness. She said she was grateful to have had all the things she's had – you in particular.' Mack turned and put an arm around her. 'She asked me to take care of you,' he said.

'And what about your own life?'

'We don't have to talk about that now. I said I would.'

Later that night Dorothy Clay slipped into a coma; the local minister came and said the last rites over a sputtering candle. He annointed her forehead, and he and Mack and Ann said the Lord's Prayer. By dawn she was dead. Ann proceeded numbly, doing all the things that have to be done when someone dies – the things society has provided to keep the survivors busy. She called the funeral home and welcomed the men in black suits when they arrived in their station wagon to take her mother's body away on a covered stretcher. She called the police department and reported the death. She called the funeral director and discussed arrangements. She placed a call to her father in Rome and asked one of his assistants to ask him to call her. She made a list of relatives and friends to be called, and she asked Scott's secretary to call Scott. She called the newspapers.

'Hey,' she said to Mack, when she noticed he was still there at lunchtime. 'You're going to lose your job.'

'This is more important,' he said.

'It's nice, having you here,' she acknowledged.

The funeral was on the first icy day of the year. Everyone crowded into St. Timothy's on Church Street, and the minister delivered a little eulogy about how everyone who had known Dorothy Clay had been touched by her generosity of spirit. Ann read from Romans in the Bible, 'What shall we say then to these things? If God be for us, who can be against us?'

They all sang hymns. The church was full. There were chrysanthemums everywhere. Afterward they filed out to the churchyard and watched as the coffin was lowered by pulleys into the hole that had been prepared for it under a big beech tree.

'Ashes to ashes, dust to dust,' the minister said. The women shivered and hugged themselves in their furs, and the minister dumped some gray ashes from a vial onto the coffin as it went down.

Ann sat next to her father in the front pew, but it was Macklin Riley who stood next to her when they filed out to the cemetery, and who herded her away from the newspaper reporters, and Macklin Riley who finally drove her home.

Adam Clay sat at the front of the church, but except for Ann he was surrounded by friends he had brought with him. Kate had thought she might introduce herself, but there was never a moment when he was alone. He seemed to be the magnetic center of power, a center which left his daughter alone and uncared for, making her fend for herself. Kate caught glimpses of him through the crowd, his broad, red face composed in a mask of sympathy, or thrown back in a guffaw of laughter. The sun beat through the high windows, and there was the smell of furniture polish and dust. Afterward she and David drove home in silence. She was grateful for the warmth of the car, the comfort of David's presence. For the first time in a long time, Kate felt herself relax and peer out of the world of her own fantasies and agonies into the outside. In the city, there were lighted trees on Park Avenue and Christmas decorations on Fifth Avenue, store windows draped in red and green and even an early Santa Claus standing and ringing his bell on 86th Street as night fell.

· 54 ·

Kate waited for Mack Riley outside the hospital on a winter afternoon. Inside, through the glass doors, she saw doctors and nurses chatting and a patient in a wheelchair, but she stood at the curb, winding a scarf around her neck against the cold winds gusting up East End Avenue from the river. Riley finally burst through the doors, twenty minutes late and wearing a raincoat, and they turned to walk toward the park. Kate hoped he was cold.

It was after four-thirty now and she was nervous about time. She had told David she would meet him downtown at six-thirty, although she wished, even now, that Riley would want to spend more than an hour with her. She didn't want to say no to him, but she didn't want to keep David waiting. They talked about the weather and the hospital and nothing at all as they walked downtown and into the park, past the sailboat pond and across the bottom of the Great Lawn. At the end of the largest baseball diamond, deserted in the cold twilight, they walked up the steps to the Belvedere, a turreted castle perched on rocks above the lake. Leaves blew across the flagstones. The wind sent cold shafts through Kate's coat. It would soon be dark. The park was dangerous at night.

'You're cold.' Mack put an arm around her as she shivered, and they leaned over the parapet to look down at the lake. In the fading light it was medieval and romantic, the garbage and old tires at the edge of the shore merged with the shadow of the reeds. One duck struck out from the farther side, leaving a wake of soft ripples.

'I guess we should start back,' Kate said. It already looked dark down in the trees they had to walk through to get back to Fifth Avenue.

'I have to go back to work, but let's stay a minute.' Although she had been anxious about saying no to Mack, now she was upset that she didn't have to. It was always the same with him. Let's meet, but I have to go. Come here, but keep your distance. Tonight they'd be back with time to spare before she had to meet David. She began to look forward to dinner, the restaurant, their friends, and David's quiet loyalty. As night fell, the cold seemed to seep up from the stones and through the soles of her shoes. She shivered again.

'This is hard to say,' Mack began, as he guided her down the steps and away from the castle with its view of the lake. 'I am going to try and be honest with you. I still think we should go on being friends.'

'But—'

'That's just it, but I . . .'

'What?'

'I don't think we should get too involved, you know, physically. It's nothing to do with how I feel about you.'

'What is it to do with?' she asked. Mack didn't answer her. 'I thought you were going to be honest with me,' she said.

'It's to do with other people, my job.'

'Who then?'

'It's that it makes such a difference to me when we do, when we did, I mean.' They had reached the sailboat pond and walked with faster steps toward the entrance to the park. The street lamps were on, and they cast an eerie glow on the asphalt path. She thought she saw the shadow of someone following them behind the trees.

'How much of a difference?' she asked.

'This much.' It was dark now, and Riley held his arms wide apart to measure the distance, his feelings for her, what he was giving up. They were at the gate to the park on Fifth Avenue.

'It's Ann.' Kate stopped at the edge of the sidewalk.

'Yes,' he said, 'Ann is part of it.'

'I *knew* it!'

· 235 ·

'Well then, you knew before we did.'

'Is she separated from Scott yet?'

'She will be in a week or two.'

'When did it start, I mean, were you stringing us both along the whole time, were you sleeping with both of us all along?' Kate was angry now, and she resisted Riley's move uptown. She would make him late.

'Ann and I haven't made love,' he said. 'That's not what it's like.'

'What *is* it like?' Kate was relieved and incredulous.

'It's a very deep friendship, a very deep involvement, and a lot of admiration.'

'And a lot of money, and a lot of power.'

'Katie!'

'You can't avoid it. Don't you see what kind of decision you're making? That family will *own* you, you'll be their pet doctor, just like Scott was their pet tennis pro. That kind of money makes everything different.'

'I've thought about that, I don't think that's what's behind this. Perhaps I can use the money to do some good things.'

'You'll never get fired now, you'll have your own lab, your own battalion of research assistants. It's a good deal for you, isn't it?'

'You're so angry.'

'Of course I'm angry,' Kate burst out. They had turned up Fifth Avenue and Kate realized from a soreness in her throat that she was yelling. Yelling to be heard over the roar of traffic and the belch of buses and just yelling because she felt like it. 'You're right I'm angry. Jesus! Here you were, letting us both think we would end up with you, jerking us both around. You slept with me, even though you knew you shouldn't have, and not just once! Don't you think that meant anything to me? Do you think you can just walk away from that, and I'll smile and say thank you, Doctor? I mean what were you thinking? What were your motives?'

Her outburst silenced Riley for a minute. 'I don't know,' he said, when he answered. 'Maybe I didn't think. I don't think that much, you know, I just go from day to day. I know it sounds funny, but when I'm at work, I don't worry about anything but work – and most of the time I'm at work. That's bad, I guess. I was just very attracted to you. I knew we shouldn't, but somehow it seemed all right. Maybe you convinced me. At the same time my friendship with Ann was deepening, growing. I didn't think about how it would seem to you. I'm sorry you see it that way.'

'You didn't think, great, you just acted. Is that what doctors do?'

'Doctors are just like everyone else, Kate. Listen, can I ask you something? To me, making love to you was pleasant, but I have the feeling it meant more than that to you. What did you expect from me, what did you think would happen?'

They had turned east now, and Riley's question stopped Kate for a moment in front of a brownstone with a long stoop coming down the street. A tree in its yard swayed in the cold wind.

'I don't know what I expected,' Kate said. What had she thought? That she would leave David and marry Riley and have his child? And what had she to go on? One nice afternoon and a little innuendo? 'I guess I thought you were going to take care of me somehow,' she said. 'I thought you were going to take care of me.'

'Take care of you! How on earth could I do that? I'm just separated from my wife of fifteen years, my job's in trouble, I'm very depressed about my medical skills, as you know. What made you think I could take care of you, when I can barely take care of myself?'

'I wanted you too much,' Kate said. But it wasn't Riley she had wanted, she saw now, but someone in a white coat with its promise of protection, salvation, and cure – someone in authority who would stand between her and the dreadful uncertainties of real life.

'I'm sorry,' he said.

'Are you sure you're making the right decision? Ann's stronger than she seems now, you know. All that money, all that power, I'm afraid they'll roll right over you and your good intentions.'

'I don't know, I don't know the answers, Kate. Maybe I'm looking for security or someone to take care of me. I don't ask myself questions like that unless I'm talking to you.'

'I guess I should be flattered,' she said. 'Are you going to get married?'

'Probably after Christmas. Ann wants her father to be here, and we have to wait until the divorce is final.' They were approaching the hospital and Riley slowed his pace. 'One thing I do know is that we all have to make decisions. Making the wrong one is better than not making them at all. Maybe this is wrong, maybe it's wrong for Ann. It doesn't matter that much.' Riley was squeezing her hand, and her wedding ring was pressed against the flesh so hard that by the time they reached the corner the flesh felt raw above the kunckle. Kate reached up to suck at the sore spot.

'I've wounded you,' he said.

'You've wounded me.' But she felt whole, not wounded. Riley was a man just like the rest of them, and she wanted too much from men. If she had been with him, she would have been disappointed, the way she was always disappointed. It was her disappointment that made trouble. He wouldn't have made the difference; no one could. He wouldn't have taken away the bright dreams that caused her discontent.

'Katie,' he drew out the syllables of her name. 'I don't want to hurt you, I don't want to hurt anyone.'

'It's all right,' she said, and she reached up to kiss his cheek. 'Really, we'll still be good friends,' and she turned and walked down the dark street, past the Chinese restaurant and the lights of an antique store, past the bar called the Recovery Room. When she got to the corner and stopped on the curb to wait for the light to change, she turned around. He was still standing and watching her as she walked away. When the light changed, she waved to him and crossed the street toward home.

· 55 ·

Kate walked across the lawn and jumped over the flower bed and into the pine woods. The lilac bushes at the edge of the woods were heavy with fragrant lavender plumes. She walked on the springy carpet of needles up the slight incline behind the house. Through the trees she could see the flowering quince hedge and the willows on the other side of the brook. She slumped down into the warm indentation of her sitting stone. In the woods there was the chirping of spring warblers and the long call of the bobwhite. Beyond that she could hear the sounds of boxes being dragged over the gravel and heavy doors slamming, as the furniture and contents of the house were moved out and loaded into the big moving van.

She had been down there helping with David all morning, sorting out the books and treasures she wanted to move to New York, and consigning piles of her past – old photographs, old school art projects, broken furniture – to the trash. She and David had cleaned out the attic and her old bedroom and her father's study, while Don Anderson directed the whole operation in a way that made the movers grumble and slow down.

Her mother had sold the house. It was a year now since she had been diagnosed as having cancer, and Kate had gone to Parkinson Center with her pathology and met Dr. Riley, and all that had happened. Her mother's chances of never having a recurrence were improving every day. Don Anderson had been offered a job teaching yoga in Florida, and her mother had decided to go with him. She was right – it was time for a change.

Kate had always been frightened at the idea of her childhood home being sold. She had thought that throwing out the junk in the attic would be throwing out the past itself. She had thought she needed the house, that without it she would be nobody. She had thought she needed someone to take care of her. But as she relaxed against the stone and looked up at the sky, she felt relief instead of sadness. Now she could start her own life; now she was no longer a child.

Two trees away, a squirrel hopped along the piny floor of the woods, avoiding the sticky cones which had fallen during the winter. Kate sat perfectly still. The squirrel hopped closer, cocking its head to watch her. Coming closer, it pushed a sharp nose at the edge of her sneaker and then hopped away. The woods and trees were full of life, life which would go on season after season, unruffled by the little dreams of men and women. The sun felt warm on Kate's head and shoulders, and she sat there and remembered all the other times she had fitted her body into the stone's comforting indentation. This was the last time.

After a while, Kate stood up, stretched, breathed deeply, taking in the thick scent of pitch and pine, and walked back to the house.